Praise for *From Bin to Banquet!*

Vicki is genuine person who honestly cares about your health and well-being. Her book, *From Bin to Banquet* just makes sense. If you think about all of the "junk" that we put into our bodies its no wonder that we have issues with it working properly. I've only read half of the book so far and I have learned so much and I have had several "now I get it" moments all ready. Come to it with an open mind and it will help you too.

—*Melissa*

I have tried other transitional programs in the past but none can come close to the one that Vicki Talmage has written in *From Bin to Banquet* in terms of convenience and effectiveness; I have had incredible results from following her program. It will be easy to continue to incorporate a healthy lifestyle into my busy life.

—*Laura*

The Vitae products helped me overcome sugar and starch cravings. I felt great during my colon cleanse, I did not feel hungry. For many years to satisfy what I thought was hunger I ate sugary and starchy foods. Now I realize that it was not hunger but cravings. It's great to feel in control without these cravings.

—*Jolynn*

D1475001

Vicki is the complete personification of what she teaches in her book. She learned the principles by healing her own health challenges. For the last 26 years she has taught those living principles to others. Her reputation is impeccable. People from all over the globe seek her out for her extensive research and her high level of radiant vitality, energy, and well being. Her book is written in a sequential, easy-to-follow form that shows the *what, why,* and *how* of gaining increased health and energy by eating raw, enzyme-enriched food. Delicious recipes are included to keep the raw food program both delicious and interesting. *From Bin to Banquet* goes far beyond being a guide for a healthier body, as it also opens the way to heal oneself mentally, emotionally, and spiritually.

This has made me feel alive again! I have so much energy, and my memory is as good as in my youth. I am never hungry, and I feel satisfied as I eat more healthy foods. I concentrate better at work, which is so important!

I read your book in one day! It was fascinating and so logical. I was impressed with you commonsense approach to nutrition. I have implemented many of your suggestions into my diet. Almost immediately I have realized increased vitality and a greater sense of well-being. Thank you for putting into writing your valuable insights.

—Name withheld

VICKI TALMAGE
From Bin to Banquet

Contact us to receive a free catalog
of current and upcoming products and books
by Vicki Talmage and *VitaeLife!*

VitaeLife!
115 East 7200 South
Midvale, Utah 84047
(801) 205-5222
www.VickiTalmage.com
Vicki@VickiTalmage.com

VICKI TALMAGE
From Bin to Banquet

Bring Your Food Alive!
Sprouting, Growing and Using Living Foods

Cover design by Douglass Cole; Cole Design
Typesetting by Brian Carter; SunriseBooks.com
Editing by Larry Barkdull

115 East 7200 South
Midvale, Utah 84047
(801) 205-5222
Vicki@VickiTalmage.com

The views expressed in this book do not supercede
prudent medical care. The reader, knowing his/her
unique medical and mental condition is responsible to
consider all information contained in this book with
care suggested by medical professionals.

Second Printing: July 2006

ISBN: 0-9779190-0-5

Contents

Eat It Raw. Let's Get Started!

Maintaining and sustaining good health is our most valuable achievement--the foundation to enjoying and accomplishing all other life pursuits.

Living Foods, Living Cells, Vibrant Life!

Age is not a matter of how many years you have, but the integrity of your body's cells.

Enzymes are the Missing Link

Enzymes are the life force of the cell and the driving force of energy in living foods for renewal of the human body.

Sprouted Foods are Super Foods

Sprouts are super foods containing the maximum vitamin, mineral and enzyme capacities to cleanse, heal and regenerate cells.

List of Recipes

Chapter 13

Foreword

For the past twenty years, my clients have asked me—well, hounded me—to gather my teachings and recipes into a book that follows the seminars I teach.

"Where can I buy a book that has this information and has some easy recipes to get started?"

Well I did it! You needed it and I needed to share it. So I took some really complicated information, chewed it up, digested it, used it to heal myself, and now I give it to you—principles that are simple, duplicatable and repeatable.

If you can listen to and hear the education that has inspired my life change, then if you will remain open-minded and draw your own conclusions for your own body and lifestyle, and then if you can watch me (or imagine watching me) throw raw vegetables into a blender and make something healthy to eat, and *then* if you can taste it and experience the shock of delicious flavor burst in your mouth that travels through your entire body...then you will discover the power and value of the simple elegance of raw-living food.

And—oh joy!—maybe you will catch the vision of your being able to manage *your own* lifestyle, and you will want to start throwing anything that's alive in *your* blender, and creating your *own* recipes, and sharing with me your own *unique* flavors and combinations of foods; and maybe you will want to start *teaching* others about your discoveries...well, it doesn't get any better than that!

I acknowledge all of those people, including medical and science experts, who have inspired me to take responsibility for my health and to live life with more beauty and meaning. Thank you for *sharing* what worked for you with me. The information and the recipes in this book were inspired by a chain of people who have been there for me, in one way or the other, during the *dark* times when I grappled for my life and some semblance of sanity in insane circumstances. You are dear to me. I could pay you no greater compliment that passing on what you gave to me.

For those of you who are now in my life—right here and now...today, please give yourself permission to consider the principles in this book and try them on for size. Add your own unique flavor. Experiment, adjust, fix them up, and, for the sake of your good health, use them! Then, when you are convinced, pass on what has worked for you.

All of us are really in this together. I am anxious to read *your* book someday, and to learn from *you*. So ahead of time, I thank you for inspiring *me* to accomplish this work. In the future, I look forward to learning from you. Feel free to add your own chapter!

Vicki Talmage

Glossary of Product Names

Expeller Pressed Oil: Like it sounds, this oil was expressed without heat. It is a *more pure* oil. It is not hydrogenated, which would be like pounding a square peg into a round hole. And the body would have to store the excess. The body can use this oil and eliminate it easier.

Nama Shoyu: *Nama* means raw, *shoyu* is soy sauce. This is the raw-food version of Kikkoman Soy Sauce. It gives fullness of flavor.

Sweeteners: Everyone has their own reason for using their sweeteners of choice. Use the one that works for you. You can substitute these three for any sweetener you enjoy:
- **Raw honey:** uncooked honey. Usually, to soften it up, set it on the counter in the sun or in the sink in warm water.
- **Pure Grade B Maple Syrup:** The Grade B pure syrup is the highest quality. Usually found on the shelf at the health food store; sometimes it is found in the refrigerated section.
- **Soaked Dates:** Soaked whole in water overnight until soft. Make sure that you take the pits out before you use them!

Veganaise: A mayonnaise-type dressing that has no milk, cheese, or eggs in it. It is a good *transition food* to prepare you for more raw foods. You find it in the refrigerated section of the health food store. There is only one problem with this:

Don't eat it with a spoon; it's too good! *Follow your Heart* is the brand name.

Bubbies: A brand of condiments, claiming that they are raw sauerkraut and pickles, and horseradish. Again, these foods assist you to transition more easily into the raw food realm.

Spike: A seasoning of herbs that assists in the transition process. Use instead of salt. Modern Products, Inc, is the manufacturer.

Real Salt: A direct mineral, mined from the Redmond Salt Mine in Central Utah. It is a pure source of salt, and pink in color as well. It contains no colorings, bleach or additives. Redmond Minerals, Inc. is the manufacturer.

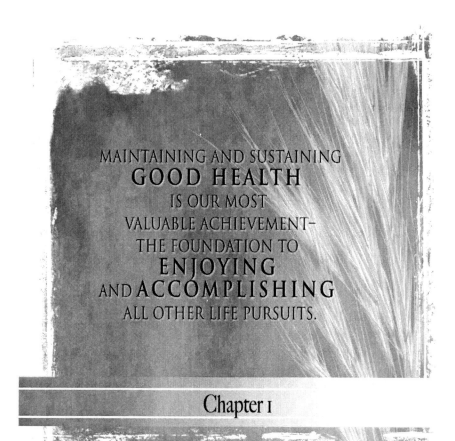

MAINTAINING AND SUSTAINING
GOOD HEALTH
IS OUR MOST
VALUABLE ACHIEVEMENT–
THE FOUNDATION TO
ENJOYING
AND ACCOMPLISHING
ALL OTHER LIFE PURSUITS.

Chapter 1

Eat It Raw. Let's Get Started!

So how can you create good health in the midst of life's craziness? There's a good chance that you have what you need in your basement or garage. In fact, some of you probably have enough and to spare. Grains, seeds, nuts—you know, that stuff that you may have stored away years ago and have never touched.

What have you been saving all that food for?

When were you planning to use it?

Is it still good?

How are you going to use it?

Some of you may not have *anything* in your house, let alone something healthy! Maybe you are getting tired of eating out and putting up with the heartburn. You may need to lose some added weight. If you choose to practice some prevention and change even part of your diet to healthy, cellular-building foods, it can only be a benefit to you. Whatever your situation may be, it has been my experience that learning how to prepare healthy, delicious meals can create sustained energy, clarity, strength and permanent health.

It won't happen to me, will it?

It could be time to implement a few simple steps and get organized while we are living in a time of health, peace and prosperity...*before* a crisis hits. Today is the time to learn to use nutrients from grains, nuts, seeds, legumes and honey, as well as water, salt and oils. As you begin to use what you have on hand, you may wish to replace it with some better quality oils, salt, and water to achieve *optimum nutrition* that you will need now and in the future.

Management of your personal food supply should be part of any emergency reserve; it is as important as saving some money for a rainy day. Food management is so much more than saving for a catastrophic event; you can cut back on your food budget by shopping for bulk items in season and look for those things that are on sale.

Poisonous chemicals and additives in foodstuffs coupled with convincing advertising campaigns, secure profits for food manufacturers. Artificially preserved foods increase their shelf life, and diminish expensive refrigerated units to keep food fresh. These poisonous substances, although usually approved for public consumption, can cause severe health problems and allergies.

Health issues, either your own or those of a loved one, can dramatically affect your capacity to create an income. However, food management can also help to soften times of incapacitation. You can draw from your food reserve until your health improves and you are back to work, without skipping a beat. Expect the unexpected.

Dishonesty and greed in business caused by bad employees and business partners, unwise business decisions you have made, or simple downsizing at your place of work, can jeopardize your income or cost you your job. How are you going to eat, and feed your family?

Selfishness in relationships, especially in marriage, where partners and children are depending on each other for financial well being, can negatively affect your marital status *and* your economic support system.

Any of these and other conditions can send you into a financial tailspin. In this day and age, the likelihood of each of us experiencing at least three major financial crises in our lifetime is a reality. The chance of one of these events happening to you is more likely than experiencing a natural disaster. For any unexpected catastrophe, you will need optimum nutrition for mental, physical and emotional stability. You can expect stress, so any previous preparation that has helped you to establish good habits will pay off by keeping the home front as simple and normal as possible.

Ask yourself, how much more difficult and stressful would a crisis be if you had to *suddenly* learn to use what food you have on hand in order to survive? My own experience has taught me that it can be tough, especially when your mind is forced to be in survival mode, to even think about eating or feeding your family. It is nice to have on hand foods that you have already integrated into the family diet. What a comfort to create healthy meals, without even thinking about each step, because it's already a habit.

In healing the body, it is much easier to *prepare and prevent* than to try and catch up during a tragedy. In times of peace and plenty we could choose today to plan ahead and integrate healthy and wise practices so we can work out the kinks and modify our plan *before* a crisis hits.

What is *Living Food?*

Living food is alive. It is rich in enzymes, which are important to digest foods and break up aggregated substances that the body stores. Living enzymes are vital to assist the body in protecting itself from disease. History is replete with diseases decimating communities for the lack of fresh live foods. Clearly, living foods are the vital key to optimum health. Living foods are our highest source of ready-to-use vitamins and minerals. In fact, the body readily absorbs minerals through the photosynthesis process—from plants. Plants and greens are our greatest source of fresh, absorbable minerals and vitamins; they are the most economical foods, the most valuable to your body, and the easiest foods to grow.

How do I create *plants* from grains, nuts and seeds?

Here's the answer: by soaking then sprouting them. As the germination process begins and the seed starts to grow, the seed goes through different nutritional stages. The *soaking stage* where the seed begins germination, the *growing stage* where you begin to see a little tail grow, the *green stage* where chlorophyll is introduced and a small stem forms, the *stem stage* where the stem is prominently thick, the *leafing stage* where the stem becomes a blade of grass or begins to grow leaves, and the *jointing stage* where we want the "green or grass" to be harvested and used.

As we recognize these stages we can understand the different ways and times to use the sprouts, greens, or grasses.

Another benefit to soaking and sprouting is unlocking the sprout's valuable *living protein amino acids* and the essential *electrolytes*. These nutrients power up the body in times of crisis, and they diminish wear and tear on our organ systems when we eat them everyday. Sprouts are already predigested and therefore use much less energy for the body to absorb and assimilate, giving quick and steady sustainable energy. Less wear and tear on the body slows down the aging process and gives valuable energy to your organs and cells to repair and regenerate them. Living food storage means that you have available the grains, seeds and nuts, which you can soak and sprout in order to create quick, concentrated nutrition, along with better clarity for your mind and usable energy for your body. Having the right equipment handy means you can easily integrate this healthy food into your daily food preparation habits.

What if I have no space? How can I manage even small food supplies?

If you don't have much space to store extra foods, you can always rearrange a cabinet, closet, or even use plastic storage boxes or buckets to store and rotate grains, nuts and seeds. Remember, you will be sprouting and using these every week to add to your daily meals.

Note: If you are storing grains, nuts and seeds in cans, use CO_2 packing instead of Nitrogen packing so the grains have life to be sprouted. Be sure to date the cans and use the oldest ones first as you rotate and replenish your storage.

For everyday use, organize your grains, nuts and seeds in quart glass jars that you keep handy in a dedicated cabinet in your kitchen.

Use other containers for storing sprouted crackers, manna breads, and dried fruits and vegetables that you will use in addition to salads for your meals.

Keep your sprouting trays and seeds close to the kitchen sink for easy soaking, rinsing and harvesting cleanup.

For convenience, keep your wheatgrass juicer, Champion Juicer and blender close to your sink and sprouting cabinet.

I have no extra money. When should I start gathering a food supply?

If finances are a problem, try purchasing just a *few* pounds of grain, nuts, or seeds when you grocery shop every week, or buy only 1 box of cookies instead of three, and put the extra money towards a sprouter! I found in my own experience that when I stopped buying bulk snacks and eating out at fast food places, the money spent there easily was substituted for buying the grains, nuts, and seeds. These healthy foods will gradually become part of your rotating food reserve that you use everyday, so they shouldn't put a dent in your food budget.

Take advantage of the fall harvest when prices are low and grains, nuts and seeds are fresh and plentiful. Whenever possible buy organic foods. They have nutrients and minerals that are not found in commercially grown and processed foods. In a crisis situation, these high quality foods can offset stress by keeping your body alkalized, and add natural antioxidants to scavenge the free radicals that can quickly cause your health to degenerate.

Remember, any living food that you can add to meals, including snacks, will enhance the quality of your body's cells, resulting in healthy-looking skin, stronger body and bones, better mental clarity, increased energy and vitality, and a feeling of well being. Why not begin feeling this way today?

How do I get started?

Step #1. Ask yourself, "What food stuffs do I have on hand? What meals can I make with what I already have?" Use up what you already have in the house, write down as many different meals as you can think to create, whether they are healthy or not.

Step #2. Take an inventory. "What grains, nuts, seeds, and legumes do I have on hand that I can soak and sprout *now* to create *enzyme-alive foods?*" These will give the body living enzymes, nutrients, and roughage to *balance* out each meal. Add these living foods to your meals that you are already eating. Integrate the healthy foods as you use up the processed foods that you may be used to. Few people can 'cold turkey' into a healthier lifestyle. To make healthy meals more of a permanent habit, do what it takes to get the 'good stuff' down. You will naturally make healthier choices as you go along, especially if you don't feel like you are forced to. In my own experience, this transition can be much smoother in times of peace and *choice* rather than waiting until a crisis forces you to make the change.

Step #3. Begin practicing soaking and sprouting these foods. Snack on them as they are growing. Add them to your salads (which are to be eaten first in the meal), dressings, nut butters and blender drinks. You can even eat them plain! Don't worry if you waste batches in the beginning. Give yourself the permission to learn. Keep trying. Soon you will perfect your own method of *personal kitchen gardening*, and you will reap financial *and* healthy benefits (see Chapter 5).

Here's a goal: Try to build up to **50% living raw food** with each meal. Remember to **eat the raw food first**. This will stimulate the brain that there are adequate enzymes built into the meal that you need for digestion, and it won't be necessary to steal enzymes from other organ systems.

Step #4. Choose a patch of ground to grow your seeds. Some suggestions are: large flower pots, a square-foot-garden, or growing trays with soil that you can place in your kitchen. Buy some seeds such as Swiss chard, spinach, kale or collards. These greens are easy to grow, and they are cold resistant. The "greens" provide a very nutritious *base* for your raw vegetables in your salads to be eaten at lunch and dinner. They contain ample protein and calcium for clear thinking and energy. Integrate these *power foods* into your daily diet, and, to accentuate the taste, use a variety of delicious dressings, included in this book. As an additional step, plant some root vegetables like beets and carrots, which you can keep stored in the ground or in a fridge (see Chapter 13).

Step#5. As you learn to grow, sprout and use your seeds, experiment with combinations of the greens (salads) and dressings to create your favorite tastes. Eat meals in courses: first; salads, greens, and raw vegetables then steamed or cooked vegetables, and finally any starch or protein foods. Eating the raw food *first*, stimulates the brain that the body is provided with the optimum live cellular foods that are rich with enzymes, to assist with digestion and assimilation. With living enzymes already in the meal, the stomach has the enzymes needed to digest more difficult foods (see Chapter 3).

Feel your energy increase as you make the daily choice to feed your cells correctly. Natural *cleansing reactions* may occur in your body to rid itself of residual artificial foods. This is part of the natural process for the body to cleanse itself before it can rebuild (see Chapter 4).

Step#6. Limit your shopping for groceries to just once a week. This will force you to use up what you have and keep a fresh supply on hand. Use your oils, water, honey, nuts and seeds daily. Date the containers, and use the oldest ones first.

Try purchasing grains and legumes in bulk, especially at the end of the harvest season.

Note: To test the viability of your grain; fill a quart glass jar half with grain and half with water. Let the jar sit overnight. The next morning, pour the contents into trays, cover and let the contents sprout up. Rinse again in the evening. If you can see a little growth at the end of the grain, it is alive and viable. Cover the tray and let it sit overnight again. When you rinse the contents the following morning, the growth will be longer, like a little tail. Now you know that this grain is good and you can use it. On the other hand, if you see no growth, grind up the grain and use it as flour to use in breads or concentrated starches—or just throw it out and replace it.

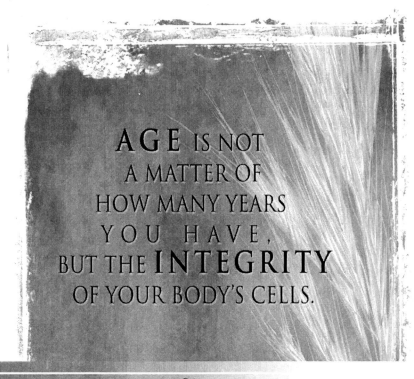

AGE IS NOT
A MATTER OF
HOW MANY YEARS
YOU HAVE,
BUT THE **INTEGRITY**
OF YOUR BODY'S CELLS.

Chapter 2

Living Foods, Living Cells, Vibrant Life!

Your age is not so much the condition of your accumulated years rather the vitality of your body's tissues. Your tissues depend on the amount of enzymes available to carry on the metabolism of every cell in your body. Many degenerative diseases can be linked to improperly digested foods and their by-products that are absorbed into the body through the bloodstream. Living foods that are packed with enzymes can help break down these toxic by-products so the body and blood can get rid of them. The extra energy can be used by the cells to regenerate themselves, which results in glowing skin, mental clarity, vibrant energy, and optimal health.

An adequate amount of enzymes means higher energy. Because more nutrients become available less food is needed. That means less digestive stress and less waste products resulting in the conservation of your energy reserves. The more digestion is accomplished in the stomach by the raw food enzymes that you have eaten, the fewer enzymes the pancreas and intestines need to produce to get the job done. You can conserve the extra energy, working with your body's metabolic processes to repair tissue, organs, and other parts of your body.

It is important to chew your food. Digestion begins when chewing starts. Take your time eating your food. If you are eating too fast, you are probably eating too much food, which can accumulate in the esophagus, causing heartburn and reflux symptoms. It is hard to over-eat living foods in their natural state. The abundance of enzymes in live raw foods can assist in breaking up the accumulated sludge in the esophagus, and pass it through the body. Eat the raw living food first.

Sprouts are life-generating foods

Uncooked vegetables and greens are full of chlorophyll, which is the most absorbable medium through which minerals can be successfully transported to the body's cells. Greens and plants, therefore, are the most beneficial of biogenic foods, because they contain agents called phytonutrients. These agents can fight cancer and other degenerative diseases because they help prevent cellular disorganization. Chlorophyll is a neutralizer that disarms carcinogens—cancer-causing agents—and prevents the cells from mutating when they are under attack. For example: a phytonutrient found in broccoli—sulphoraphane—functions as an *activator* for a group of enzymes that will attach itself to harmful carcinogens and carry them safely out of the cells. Another example is cabbage that contains oltipraz, which increases enzyme production and protects the colon, bladder, liver, lung, breast, stomach, and skin against cancers.

I have studied some of the scientists who have believed and lived this way of life. I am impressed at their youthful and vibrant appearances. They have the energy to make great contributions even in their advancing years.

One scientist discovered that the optimal cellular foods for the body are fruits, vegetables, and whole grain--mainly sprouted. These foods should not be eaten in abundance; rather they are fuel to be eaten in amounts that would still feed the cells while you might feel as if you were close to starvation. The scientist experimented with white mice, which, he discovered, lived substantially beyond their normal life expectancy. Furthermore, the parents produced healthier offspring in their later years, than they had in their earlier years.

The scientist lived this program as well. As I watched his filmed thesis, I was impressed with the tautness of his skin, his thick silver hair, his crystal blue eyes, and the strength of his muscles as he ran in knee-deep water on the beach. I was in my early 20s then. His research inspired me to integrate these foods exclusively in my diet. Over the years I have experienced similar results: my body has grown healthier because I consistently followed this diet. I am the mother of seven children. With each birth, the child's weight was better and he/she was healthier than the last. Additionally, my health continued to improve, and each birth was easier. I was able to use no pain relievers.

I was intrigued by another scientist's experiment using these principles. He managed to keep a chicken's heart alive by releasing its wastes everyday. The heart lived for about 25 years until a technician neglected to perform the cleansing procedure and the heart became auto-intoxicated. When the waste had been removed on a regular basis, the heart could regenerate itself. We must ask ourselves the questions: Could that happen to our bodies as well? Could my cells regenerate if I ate in a manner that didn't create so much waste? Inspired by this research, I began to cleanse my body on a quarterly basis; I ate more living foods so my body wouldn't collect and recycle the wastes. This research has inspired the work that I do today.

There are many extraordinary people around the world, especially in television and theater, who have quietly embraced this lifestyle and manifest still, the glow of health and vigor in their older years. Their examples have intrigued and inspired me to integrate these principles into my life. The results are still astounding.

As I have continued to study about living foods, sprouts, and wheatgrass juice, a common denominator appeared: *light.* I discovered that there is more light, oxygen and energy in living foods. Why? Because of the chlorophyll content in these foods, which is liquid oxygen and liquid light. Through the photosynthesis process, light is transformed from its source, which is the sun, into the foods that we eat, through the medium of chlorophyll. The chlorophyll carries the "light" from the sun to living foods for us to ingest and use. That same light, changed enough so we can assimilate it,

ignites enzymes, feeding our cells to manifest health
throughout our entire system.

> "Absorption and organization of sunlight, the
> very essence of life, is almost exclusively derived
> from plants. Plants are therefore a biological
> accumulation of light. Since light is the driving
> force of every cell in your bodies, that is why we
> need plants." (Dr. Klinic Bircher-Benner)

Free Radicals and Antioxidants

Free radical damage, caused by disease, normal
exercise, stress and pollutants can damage the cell at the
nuclear level. As the primary cell is attacked, it loses
one of its important molecules and cannot function
properly. As it scrambles to find another molecule it
creates a cascade effect: the damaged cell has to steal its
missing molecule from another cell, which steals from
another cell, and so on. Eventually, a weak organ in
your body is attacked and disease and degeneration
follows.

Antioxidants are the answer. Rich living foods
are the best and most economical source of antioxidants. Bottled antioxidants, even if dehydrated below
105° F, still lack the full viability of fresh, living foods.
Greens, vegetables, sprouted foods, and fruits eaten in
their natural state, have sufficient intact antioxidants to

literally scavenge the free radicals and remove them from the body through the kidneys and renal system.

Pure water

Understanding that these toxins will be carried out of the renal system and kidneys, the necessity for a gallon of pure solvent water everyday can be understood. Even it you eat a 100% living food diet you still must drink a gallon of water a day. Fresh steamed, distilled water is the obvious choice—the perfect pure solvent. Some people have claimed that steamed distilled water leeches the minerals from the body, leaving you depleted. If that is so, my stance for living foods is an effective solution. Since the body can only absorb minerals through the photosynthesis process, the best source of fresh minerals comes from greens, wheatgrass juice and organic vegetables, not from your water. Water is needed as a pure solvent, to flush these toxins out of the kidneys and renal system. Anything added to the water makes it a food, and it will pass through the digestive system, not the kidneys.

Nevertheless, the body must have pure water to rehydrate itself. Water dilutes toxins, which can then be passed more easily through the kidneys. Water fires the body's electrical and chemical processes that work hard all day to gather and release the body's most toxic waste—CO_2. (Isn't it interesting that we as a society drink 8-64 ounces of soda pop everyday, which counteracts the body's ability to release this most poisonous substance?) Eight glasses of water everyday is dedicated to firing the release of CO_2 as waste. Rehydrating the body and diluting toxins requires more water—16 glasses or 1 gallon of pure water everyday is needed, in addition to your raw living foods. Drinking 16-36 ounces of water when you wake up in the morning usually satisfies thirst and sets the body's elimination channel in motion. Drinking another quart of water during or after morning exercise satisfies the body's needs until noon. Drinking another 2 quarts of water throughout the afternoon satisfies the daily goal of one gallon.

If you discover that you are urinating a lot in the beginning, join the club! All who are serious about rehydrating the skin, body and organ systems experience this step. Keep drinking water. And remember, if anything is added to water, the body treats it like a food. Water *must* be a pure solvent to pass through the renal glands. Add nothing fibrous or flavorful. Adding anything to water will cause it to pass through the digestive tract and through the bowels. Water is at its best as a pure solvent.

Mucous forming foods

Foods such as eggs, milk, cheese, flour, pasta, too much meat and dairy products, which are mucus-forming foods accumulate over time in the small intestine and stick to the villi. The villi are the small finger-like projections in the small intestines and esophagus, which primarily absorb nutrients. Mucous forming foods and poisonous foods adhere to the villi and cause them to cling together. If you choose to decrease some of these foods in your daily diet, the first goal is to clean out the intestines, and release the villi to absorb nutrients. Then *stop* eating these mucus-forming foods and putting them back into your body!

Secondly, integrate into your diet, foods that support cellular regeneration such as fresh fruits, lots of vegetables and sprouts, and wheatgrass juice. Greens, vegetables, and sprouted foods help to alkalize the body and rid degenerative toxins from the tissues, organs, and passageways.

Here is a good goal to choose: Eat living, raw, unprocessed vegetables and sprouts for at least fifty percent of your daily food consumption. This means that you literally eat a salad, piece of fruit or vegetable before you allow yourself to eat a cookie, some candy, or a burger.

Why would this make such a difference in your health?

Every time you place something in your mouth, your brain defines what it is and if it has any enzyme content. If there are no enzymes, your brain will trigger your stomach to release enzymes to digest the food. Unfortunately, we are only born with a certain amount of enzymes, and when the stomach becomes the only source of those enzymes, they are soon depleted causing the body to *steal* enzymes from the gall bladder. (Could this be a reason why so many people are losing their gall bladders in their 20's?) After the gall bladder is depleted, enzymes are leeched from the bones and osteoporosis becomes a possibility. What a powerful prevention of osteoporosis this could be! Make sure everything that goes into your mouth is full of live enzymes that are eaten *first;* you can eat other more concentrated foods afterwards, if you choose to.

Raw foods for *life!*

The power of raw, living fruits, vegetables and sprouted foods is unlimited. The body and the cells become vibrant and alive, filled with energy. There are many creative and delicious ways that you can extract *deliciousness* from simple foods. But no matter how *gourmet* you become, always remember the basics:

- Eat a "greens" salad *before* eating more concentrated raw foods.
- Remember to drink a gallon of pure water everyday.
- Drink 4 ounces of wheatgrass juice everyday.
- Eat a piece of watermelon everyday.
- Split up your carbohydrates and your proteins, and eat them separately for each meal: one at lunch and the other at dinner, always after your greens.

- Eat you last meal before 7 p.m. to give your body a rest from digesting food.

These principles are not new. Interestingly, ancient religious documents from the dead Sea Scrolls and in the surrounding areas in a similar time period, as well as more recent documents state that plants are or should be the main staple in our diet. These documents along with modern science and my own physiological experiences have convinced me that the nucleus of our diet must become plant-based; all other foods—fruits, whole grains (mostly sprouted), and any other choices of food-types— are appendages to this nucleus.

The regenerating effect on the cells from the DNA and RNA in sprouted foods, which are highly concentrated with nutrients, produces a high concentration of vitamins, minerals, and amino acids (proteins) that feed the cells. Once cleansed first, and then regenerated by sprouted foods that are easier to digest and rich in nutrients, the body's organs *and* systems will experience a boost to the immune system, and the body's aging process will slow down—and it can.

That's good news!

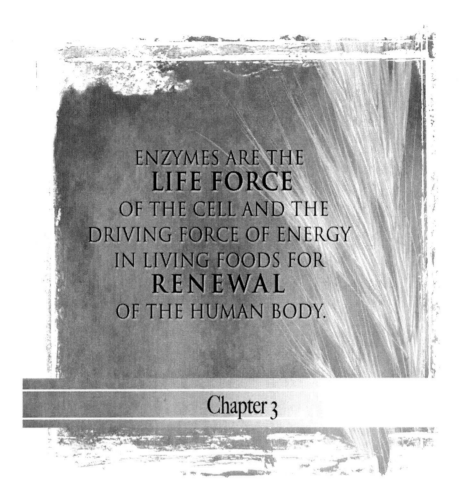

ENZYMES ARE THE
LIFE FORCE
OF THE CELL AND THE
DRIVING FORCE OF ENERGY
IN LIVING FOODS FOR
RENEWAL
OF THE HUMAN BODY.

Chapter 3

Enzymes are the Missing Link

All natural foods in their living raw state have an abundance of enzymes. Therefore, you benefit the most by eating raw foods each meal to create as many enzymes as possible. But ignorantly, we kill enzymes in raw foods:

- Cooking foods over 105° F destroys all enzyme activity. Use a dehydrator with an accurate thermometer that can be set at or below 105° F.
- Freezing food destroys the enzymes. This is evident after you remove a frozen vegetable from the freezer and thaw it out. Notice the texture of the flesh. It is soggy and lifeless because the enzymes have been destroyed.
- Too much blending or juicing at a high centrifugal force can destroy the enzymes because of the heat created by friction. When juicing, if you can use a "triturating" juicer, the enzymes can be preserved. Triturating juicers are the most expensive type of juicers, but they offer the most benefits. These juicers turn at even slower speeds or RPM's, resulting in even less oxidation from foam and less destruction of nutrients from the heat. A triturating juicer first chops the vegetable into small pulp-like pieces then squeezes out the juice through an auger-like press separating the juice from the pulp. This process keeps most of the live enzymes in tact. Mine is called a Champion Juicer and there are many more uses to this juicer than just for juice (see Chapter 6).
- Leaving out of the fridge previously cut fruits or vegetables exposes them to oxygen and the enzymes are destroyed. You will notice the browning color. Cover it well and refrigerate leftover raw foods. Use

marinates with live raw vinegars and/or lemon juice to neutralize the effects of oxidation and to extend the storage life of vegetables and fruits. When juicing raw fruit and vegetable juices, drink as soon as possible, to avoid too much oxidation. If you must store fresh juices throughout the day, be sure to cover them tightly and store them in a refrigerated environment in order to preserve as many fresh enzymes as possible. Wheatgrass juice is an exception; after wheatgrass has been pressed, it must be used immediately. Wheatgrass cannot be saved without compromising its enzyme content and its taste.

How can you know if enzymes are fresh and viable?

Here is a simple test: If the seed can sprout and grow, then all the enzymes are intact. Enzymes in such foods will leave you feeling refreshed and satisfied. These naturally building foods will first cleanse the body or system then they will build and replenish. Remember, your body does not build upon garbage; your body first wants to rid itself of the garbage then bring itself to a state where it can truly build health. This process may make you feel the cleansing reactions of the enzymes at work. Continue drinking plenty of water to dilute the toxins and *allow* your body to cleanse.

Enzyme reserves and depletions

There are two types of enzymes: *exogenous* (found in living raw foods) and *endogenous* (those produced in our bodies). The more exogenous enzymes we eat the less our bodies must borrow from the stomach, gall bladder, and bones. Enzymes in raw foods aid in digestion from the moment you begin chewing that first bite of food.

Nature placed enzymes in foods to aid in the digestion process, not to force the stomach to do all of the work. At birth, we inherited an enzyme reserve that can be depleted over time by our enzyme-deficient diet of overcooked, over-processed commercial fast foods. This enzyme reserve was designed to kick in when there aren't enough live enzymes already built into the meal. Endogenous enzymes were not meant to be used at every meal. Moreover, most of us were raised without eating ample raw foods. Remember, half of everything we eat should be living and raw. But we load our systems with burgers, fries, shakes, and over processed foods. Most people have depleted their stomachs' enzyme reserves by a young age by not including any raw living foods in each of their meals. As a result, they experience painful stomachaches, cramps, diarrhea, constipation, and myriad other digestion-related ailments. This enzyme reserve can be protected if we would eat at least 50% fresh raw foods, including vegetables, fruits and sprouted foods. Enzymes that are already present in raw foods are absorbed easily into the intestines. They are then utilized in the metabolism process, preventing more enzyme depletion and providing usable energy. This energy can be used to burn excess fat, boost your tolerance for stress, and help to heal your body systemically (see Chapter 7).

Small price, big reward

Interestingly, you can live on a cooked-food diet for many years until cellular enzyme exhaustion occurs, which weakens the immune system, creates disease, lowers energy levels, and can cause you to be overweight. Even if we can get away with it for awhile, common sense should tell us that an everyday assault of cooked foods will catch up to us. But, if you will simply begin to add raw foods to every meal, you will feel your body rewarding you with increased energy, clarity of thought and improved health...in a short period of time!

The enzymes in raw foods will digest most of the living raw food without the help of enzymes secreted by the body, and then the body can use the resulting excess energy to upkeep non-essential organ functions such as hair, skin and nails. Additionally, the master or pituitary gland, which produces its *own* human growth hormone, can utilize the unused enzymes to heal itself and to slow down the aging process...naturally.

How enzymes work

One of the major functions of enzymes is to digest foods and break them down into small particles that can easily pass through tiny pores of the intestines and enter the bloodstream for assimilation and for the absorption of nutrients. Chewing, or mastication, is the first stage of digestion. Thus, you should chew each bite *thoroughly* to aid in breaking up the food and to releases the foods' enzymes. Some people, who are advocates of eating raw foods, erroneously think that blending up the raw greens and vegetables and drinking rather than chewing them is enough. Think about this! Even if you "chew your juice," you cannot replace the benefit of the process of grinding and tearing with your molars, which is necessary to release salivary enzymes. Nothing can take the place of chewing properly. Ultimately, juicing is appropriate for quarterly cleansing so chew, chew, and chew your food in your everyday meals! *Chew it 'til it's juice!*

The enzymes break down and digest the food to small enough particles to be carried through the blood to the cells of the body to build muscles, glands, nerves and new blood cells. Enzymes also attack wastes and buildups of excessive foods, breaking them down for elimination. Enzymes neutralize and release poisons in the blood and the tissues. This process keeps the immune system strong, intact and prepared for any outside invasion. Enzymes assist in the elimination of carbon dioxide from the lungs and the formation of urea that is eliminated as waste in urine. Enzymes initiate all cellular activity. They break down toxic substances so the body can eliminate them without damaging organ systems. Enzymes can act upon a substance, change it into a usable substance—chemical or byproduct—and yet itself remain unchanged. Enzymes are the life energy of the cell. By initiating vitality in the cell first, that vitality can then be manifest throughout the entire body.

Clearly, enzymes act intelligently. When we assist our body by feeding it healthy amounts of cellular-building foods packed with enzymes, we are giving our body's cells high quality fuel that it needs to function at an optimum level, biologically, chemically and electrically. We experience less wear and tear on our systems; our bodies can regenerate and heal, and our aging process slows down. Replenishing and storing up our enzyme reserves produces healthier, more efficient bodies. It is most noticeable in the glowing nature of the skin. Vibrant health improves attitude resulting in a radiant lifestyle, regardless of your economic status. It *is* possible to feel more energy and vitality consistently everyday.

The problem with aggregation

In the study of microscopy, a drop of blood is prepared on a slide then placed under a microscope. In a live blood analysis, experts have discovered that enzyme-deficient people have fewer round, full-bodied cells which are able to absorb all of the nutrients and oxygen. If the cells lose their healthy shape and are smashed together, sometimes in chains, they can absorb very little oxygen or assimilate nutrients inadequately. This is called cellular *aggregation.* There are three major types aggregation: lipid (or fat) aggregation, sugar aggregation and protein aggregation.

Aggregation is dangerous. As a rule, whatever food you love and cannot live without will probably be what kills you. And that food will fall into one of these three aggregation categories: too many sugars, too many fats, or too many proteins. Think back to when you were a child: What was the food that you loved to eat and didn't stop eating? You are probably eating that same food today, and it is causing weakness at your cellular level. In microscopy, we discover the aggregations in your live blood, usually correlate with the aggregation—*impaction*—that is in your large intestine.

If the impaction is great enough to prevent adequate movement of waste from the large intestine—toxins, which gather behind the impaction, in liquid form—will be absorbed through the colon wall and pumped throughout the body in the bloodstream. This process will cause your body to recycle the very waste that it can't get rid of! You crave the foods that your body can't release. If you have struggled with cravings, this may be an answer for you, rather than believing that you have no self-control. It is difficult to fight a craving that is being pumped throughout your bloodstream. Live enzymes coupled with quarterly body cleansing can remove these blockages so you don't experience a weight plateau. (See Chapter 4. Also, this subject will be addressed in detail in Book 2 of this series.)

Fresh, live foods replete with enzymes have the capacity to break up these aggregated substances in the large intestines, and, over time, release them from the body. Quarterly body cleansings speed up the cleansing process and stabilizes energy levels in a matter of months as opposed to years, if the body is left to cleanse on its own. Eventually the impactions can be fully released so the fibrous waste *and* the poisonous toxins can be released naturally every day, rather than being recycled and reabsorbed by the body.

Other enzyme questions and answers

Are living enzymes different than enzymes that I buy in a bottle? Yes. Even if the enzymes have been dehydrated below 105° F and are labeled "raw," they have been changed from their natural state. Remember, nothing can substitute for enzymes in their original, natural, untampered-with state.

How do I get enzymes in their natural state? You must grow them yourself. In the following chapters you will learn why sprouting is the optimum way to get fresh enzymes. You will learn how to sprout, and you will learn many ways that you can extract the highest quality of enzymes from your sprouted foods. You will learn that you can integrate this process into your busy lifestyle. The energy, the clarity of thought, and the peace of mind, which are side effects of sprouting, are long term benefits worth every minute spent in its preparation.

Living enzymes truly are the missing link to optimum health.

SPROUTS ARE
SUPER FOODS
CONTAINING THE MAXIMUM
VITAMIN, MINERAL AND
ENZYME CAPACITIES TO
CLEANSE, HEAL
AND **REGENERATE** CELLS.

Chapter 4

Sprouted Foods are Super Foods

S prouted foods are considered the most nutritious of available fresh foods. These foods are filled with enzymes. No matter where you live or your economic level, you can enjoy growing and eating these living foods right from the comfort of your own kitchen.

Anyone can learn to sprout. Sprouts are the most economical source of food with the highest payoff in regard to cellular nutrition. Sprouts require small amounts of space and effort to store, grow, harvest, and manage. And sprouting is just plain fun! Sprouting is a time- and cost-effective way to eat. Dedicating a few minutes each morning and evening to care for your personal indoor garden can reward your body and mind with fresh cellular food that will keep you healthy and clear, and keep your cells youthful and strong.

The benefits of sprouts

Sprouts are fresh, organically grown foods in their natural state. Sprouts are naturally predigested, meaning that starches are already broken down into simple sugars, and proteins are already converted to amino acids. Therefore, these nutrients easily can be absorbed into the body providing quick, satisfying, long-lasting energy. Sprouts are an excellent food for sick people that struggle with degenerative disease. Sprouts can be blended into delicious pâtés and dressings that are not only satisfying and flavorful but a powerhouse of nutrition for weak systems. Preparing sprouts this way is a wonderful baby food, giving optimum nutrition to tiny bodies that are busy building bones, brain cells, muscles, and vital organs.

Just one sprouted seed, grain or soaked nut holds the potential for optimal detoxification, nourishment, repair and regeneration of your cells. Sprouts are the ultimate organic living food, and require the least amount of effort and maintenance, with harvest times between six hours up to one week. Sprouts can be grown on your kitchen counter, and need no expensive equipment.

Eating sprouts promotes deep cellular healing and emotional stability, assisting the body to use less energy for digestion. Stress levels decrease, so more energy can be diverted to provide vitality to the organs. With little or no stress, you might discover that you accomplish more in a shorter period of time. You may find that your body recovers more rapidly from the pressures of life, from physical work and exercise, and from sickness. Your body might begin to require less sleep, or you might find that you are relaxing better and *finally* getting adequate sleep. Eating living foods sends a message to your body that it can trust that you are going to take care of it. Remarkably, if your body trusts you, it can become your most valuable partner to achieve the goals you have for it. Conversely, if your body does not trust you, you will find it difficult to change anything with regard to your health.

Deciding to take the journey

In the beginning, your body needs consistency as you cleanse and reverse bad dietary habits. You must create a new brain pattern that ripples out to the nervous system and fires a new message to cells, which will cause new results. This consistency builds *trust* within your body—it can depend on you to feed, nurture and keep it safe. Your body will begin to understand that you will provide it with healthy alternatives as you make health your first priority. Soon, your body will step up to the plate; it will go to bat for you in fighting a degenerative disease, give you energy to persevere through a hard project, or shed excess weight.

As you begin this new lifestyle journey, be patient and give your taste buds time to embrace new flavors. If you are used to eating man-made sweets, breads, cookies, soda pop, and junk foods, your taste buds are probably clogged and lazy. Give your body the latitude to adjust to these new foods as you integrate them into your daily diet a little at a time. We love to eat, so experiment to suit your taste. Feel free to adjust the flavors to fit your unique palate. Try the recipes at the end of chapters for ideas about dressings and sauces that make every dish complete. You may want to overseason everything at first. But over time, you may cut out the salt or artificial flavor enhancers as your taste buds settle down. As a rule, try tasting the foods *before* salting them.

Enjoy your meals

In the beginning, some people eat 2-3 plates of greens, with raw veggies and sprouted foods at every meal. No problem! Let your body have the amounts of food that it needs. Everything will balance out in time. Don't worry about calorie content. Again, listen to your body and give it what it wants. When I lost 85 pounds in four months, I was eating more food than I ever had in my life! In fact, eating this way in abundant quantities fed my body so well that my cells finally let go of the toxins that had been stored up in the adipose tissue. The result for me was permanent weight loss.

Remember, sprouts are living foods that are rich with enzymes. As they break up blockages and attack impactions, you may experience a little gas and bloating. This is normal, and to quote a pun, "this too shall pass!" As the enzymes break up the impactions, previous improper food combining like fruits and vegetables eaten together, or starches and proteins eaten together, naturally create fermentation. During this process, the aggregated material is broken up and moved out of where it had been stored, and the trapped toxic gas escapes. You may feel relief from bloating, as areas of your intestine are cleansed. Drink lots of water to accelerate the removal of blockages and to dilute toxins.

If you discover a white film on your tongue, don't panic. Your taste buds are cleansing themselves from all the over-processed foods, additives, flavor enhancers and chemicals that you have been eating. You, and others, may find that you have sweeter breath!

As you are changing over your diet, you may choose to do a short body cleanse that is facilitated by a professional cleansing coach. This process can assist your body in diminishing the reactions that often accompany the change in diet. It is natural for your body to detoxify itself from the harmful substances that you used to eat in the past. (Call for more info.)

Miraculous transformation

A sprout is a concentrated food source in which the vitamin and protein content of the seed, legume, or raw nut increases substantially as it soaks and sprouts overnight. The chemistry of the seed changes as it soaks. The phytic acid that occurs naturally in the seed to inhibit *bug invasion,* dissolves during soaking and the germination process begins. Interestingly, many people, who are allergic to almonds, wheat, and other seeds, discover that soaking and sprouting seeds, nuts and grains, diminish or eliminate allergic reactions. (If you have a severe allergy, work *with* your health care provider, if you wish to experiment with this idea.)

Once the germination process has started and the biochemistry of the seed, nut or grain changes, it is no longer a grain, it is a vegetable. It becomes a plant, not a starch. When we use the grain, nut or seed in its dry form, and grind it to flour for use *without* soaking it, it becomes acidic. Excess acid in the body, we know creates an environment ripe for disease. On the other hand, alkaline foods, such as soaked nuts and sprouts, balance the body's pH level, which forms a healthy environment that promotes health and rejuvenation.

Remember, any food worth eating that tends to increase your health will first cleanse out toxins and acid. The body cannot build upon disease. Healthy foods such as sprouts help the body to *first* remove disease and acidity and rid itself of the excess, and then those same healthy foods will balance the pH level to alkalinity. A balance of alkalinity in the body rebuilds cellular function and points the body toward permanent optimum health.

Don't forget to drink a gallon of steam-distilled water everyday as a solvent to pull out impurities from the tissues and cells, and to re-hydrate impactions. Once re-hydrated, those impactions can be more easily released. Since water is also needed to balance the chemical and electrical reactions in the body, a gallon of pure water everyday is a must whether you are eating living foods or not. Keeping toxins diluted during times of cleansing makes the kidneys' job easier, and less will be absorbed into your bloodstream (see Chapter 2).

Sprouts and sugar

Sprouts are great for people who are diabetic, hyperglycemic, or who have challenges with their pancreas or need to keep their blood sugar levels under control. Sprouted foods are considered a *slow sugar* that supports the body as it comes off *fast sugar* cycles and high insulin levels. Most weight problems are caused by excessive sugar consumption, including fast sugars such as breads, pasta, milk products, cheese, eggs and red meats, as well as hard sugars. Sugars are addictive.

When sprouted foods are introduced to the diet, their antioxidants go right to work. They scavenge for free radicals and repair the damage that excessive consumption of fast foods has caused over the years. Your body is addicted to the level of sugar to which you have indulged.

The good news is that sprouts are rich in starches that are converted by the body into *simple sugars*, which require very little digestive breakdown, and diminish added stress on these organs. The plant starch from sprouted foods can cause less stress on the gastrointestinal tract and pancreas as opposed to the man-made starchy foods made of flour that accumulate in the digestive tract as impactions and progenerate fast sugar cycles for the pancreas.

When glycemic levels are increased with man-made starchy foods from flours, the insulin levels are again catapulted to extreme levels, which keep the adrenal glands in a "fight or flight" state. In this state, the body stores excess toxins to be used at a later time to get you through a "crisis." Toxins or fat, stored in the tissues this way, are difficult to remove, because the body begins to crave the fast sugars. If it doesn't get the fast sugars, it begins to cleanse, creating weakness, dizziness, and exhaustion—causing you to want to eat the fast sugar to satisfy the uncomfortable feelings, and so on, and so on. This is called the fast sugar cycle. Reversing it is like turning around the Titanic. It will take consistency and time to make the change, to cleanse the body and then to feed the body live-cellular building foods with sugars that are balanced and assimilable. (Addressed in the weight loss book.)

Sprouts, enzymes and proteins

Sprouts are living foods rich in enzymes. Enzymes are the living force within a substance. The protein molecule is the carrier or vehicle of the enzyme's energy. But the body needs the *proper* protein to fully utilize all that the enzyme can offer. When you soak and sprout a grain, seed or nut, the fat of it is now used to promote growth. The protein develops and is increased as the plant grows.

Proteins build bones, muscles and organs. All living, raw foods have proteins. These proteins work *with* the enzymes to produce living nutrients that feed the body at the cellular level. Many people such as athletes successfully can obtain substantial levels of protein and nutrition from a living food diet.

Many people get protein from eating meats. Typically, we cook meats at temperatures in excess of 105° F to destroy any bacterial or parasitical contamination. In the process, enzymes in the meat are killed. Eating excessive cooked meat can cause great wear and tear on the body as it struggles to find sufficient enzymes to digest it, especially if you are not eating a large "greens" salad with it. Sprouts are an excellent alternative protein source. Try adding them to your current meals. By integrating sprouted foods that have built-in, nutrients and enzymes, pure proteins are supplied to the body and nutrients are assimilated with little or nothing wasted.

Working with the body

As you introduce living foods to your daily diet, you may experience bloating, gas, headaches, weakness, and even uncontrollable cravings. These are some of the same symptoms that addicts experience in drug detoxification. If you are choosing to eat more living foods and are experiencing any of these symptoms, the solution is to be consistent. If you fall off the wagon get back on immediately. Take care of yourself by getting plenty of sleep and drinking lots of water. It is a good idea to get *colonics* during these episodes to release from the body what it can't release on its own. Quarterly body cleansing—every three months—relieves the body's reactions to cleansing as it rids itself of built-up poisons. (For more information, call office or see Book 2 in the series.)

Once you stop eating poisonous, artificial foods that are rich with chemicals, additives, colors and preservatives, you will be shocked at what you have been putting in your body. Once you are freed from the addictive clutches of these chemicals, you will be so amazed at your new, natural sustained energy, consistent clarity of mind, and your freedom from aches and pains. Be patient. Turning around fast sugar cycles can take years. Be consistent. Good habits take time. With a healthy diet and exercise, people who have not been able to previously lose weight now can manage their high blood sugar and cholesterol levels, master their sugar addictions, and drop the pounds.

Sprouted foods really *are* perfect foods.

SPROUTS ARE FOODS FOR
"LIVING CELLS".
NOURISHMENT AT THIS HEIGHT
OF REGENERATION
IS ONLY AVAILABLE
THROUGH SPROUTING.

Chapter 5

How Do I Sprout Super Foods?

Anything that can grow can be sprouted. There are many *sproutable* nuts, seeds and grains from around the world. When you travel, try different seeds and discover new flavors. The sprouting process is just the same. Take your sprouting trays with you. There are unlimited possibilities and varieties of sprouts that you can add to your diet.

There are as many ways to sprout seeds as there are people who sprout! Here is a simple process that uses inexpensive equipment. You will need glass quart jars to soak the seeds overnight; a sink with a sprayer or faucet; simple-stackable sprouting trays; and a counter or table to set them on. That's it!

How to Sprout

1. Fill a glass quart jar about half full of seeds, nuts or grains. Fill the rest of the jar with water. (You can use your purified water or you can use tap water if it isn't too polluted.)

2. Let the jar sit on the counter, uncovered, overnight, or for 8-10 hours.

3. Pour the glass jar of soaked seeds into a sprouting tray over the sink. Use the sprayer or faucet to rinse the seeds thoroughly then distribute the seeds evenly. Let them drain.

4. Cover the trays and stack them. Let them sit on the counter all day.

5. Rinse and drain the seeds again in the evening. They only need to be watered twice each day. More watering could create an environment for salmonella.

6. Repeat the process everyday, depending on how much sprouting time each grain or seed needs.

I have found that using sprouting trays with lids will keep the sprouts drained well enough to prevent them from developing bacteria, as opposed to growing sprouts in upside-down jars with screened lids, where water can get trapped and mold can grow. If you have a choice, use covered stackable-sprouting trays; you can use them over and over for a very long time.

Seeds, Grains and Legumes to Sprout in Trays 1-3 days
Follow this process for green lentils, garbanzo beans, whole peas, adzuki beans, mung beans, and any type of bean. Also alfalfa, fenugreek, wheat, rye, buckwheat, and any kind of grain.

You will notice little tails beginning to emerge from the seed within the first 24 hours. Taste them often to determine at which stage of growth is most delicious for you. They should taste sweet and desirable. Most sprouts are eaten *before* the tail gets the size of the seed or grain. To get optimum nutrition from that grain, you don't need to wait for the tail to begin to turn green. When the tail of the sprout starts to turn green, it has entered the stage to grow a stem and become a plant. This stage ultimately produces 'greens' or a grass. The time to use these sprouts is *before* the stem turns green while they are at their peak enzyme and antioxidant stage. Also, they now will be the sweetest and easiest to use in raw-food gourmet recipes.

Seeds and Legumes that Soak Overnight

These are seeds that are exceptions to the basic sprouting process above: Sunflower (hulled), pumpkin (hulled), brown sesame seeds, red lentils, flax seeds (will thicken), and any small seeds and nuts, need *only to be soaked overnight*. Drain and use these the next day. Here are instructions for these seeds:

1. Fill a glass jar about half full of seeds or nuts. Fill the rest of the jar with water—purified or tap water.

2. Let the jar sit on the counter, uncovered, overnight about 8-10 hours.

3. Pour the soaked seeds through a strainer over the sink, then use the sprayer or faucet to rinse them thoroughly. If you need to dry them, drain them on a paper towel.

4. Use the seeds that day in your salads and recipes. If you have leftover seeds, store them in an airtight bag or container in the fridge to be used within the next three days, or dehydrate any leftovers.

Seeds and Nuts that soak 4-6 hours

Here are more exceptions and instructions: pine nuts, tiny red lentils, flax seeds (not too thick), etc. The soaking time for these is substantially less.

1. Fill a glass jar about half full of seeds or nuts. Fill the rest of the jar with water—purified or tap water.

2. Let the jar sit on the counter, uncovered, overnight about 4-6 hours.

3. Pour the soaked seeds through a strainer over the sink, then use the sprayer or faucet to rinse them thoroughly. If you need to dry them, drain them on a paper towel.

4. Use the seeds *immediately* in your salads and recipes, or use them to dehydrate. These seeds are time sensitive. Try to use only what you need *now* so you don't have leftovers. They don't store well because of their delicate nature.

Soaking Larger Nuts

Yet more exceptions and instructions: almonds, Brazil nuts, filberts, walnuts, pecans, all large raw nuts need 48 hours soaking time to germinate and sprout. You may not see any outward tail, but you will notice the outward growth and swelling of the nut as the germination process is going on inside.

1. Fill a glass quart jar about half full of seeds or nuts. Fill the rest of the jar with water—purified or tap water.

2. Let the jar sit on the counter, uncovered, overnight.

3. Pour the glass jar of soaked seeds through a strainer over the sink, and use the sprayer or faucet to rinse them thoroughly. Fill the jar again with fresh water and the nuts, and once more let it sit uncovered on the counter all day.

4. Every morning and every evening repeat the same process for up to 48 hours. These nuts germinate in the water and not in the trays.

Opened nuts like walnuts and pecans will be ready in 24 hours. All other large nuts like almonds, need 48 hours to germinate. Make sure to thoroughly rinse the nuts before refilling the jar with water and allowing it to sit on the counter. You will notice a dark residual coming off the sides of the nuts, combined with the phytic acid coating and accumulating on the bottom of the jar. This residual needs to be rinsed thoroughly twice a day, for the successful germination of the nut. If you don't rinse twice a day, you may notice a rotten smell coming from the jar and the nuts will begin to go bad.

Note: Do not eat a sprouted nut, seed or grain that smells rotten or that is slimy. Throw it away and start over.

As you practice, remember to properly *rinse* your sprouts. If sprouts are left unattended for too long, they will spoil. Don't try to save the spoiling sprouts; you might get food poisoning. Just start over. The more you practice, the more you get used to caring for your sprouts.

Sprouts have taken a bad rap because the process of commercially germinating, growing, and *getting* sprouts to market on a timely schedule is almost impossible. As a result of too much time in hot trucks or refrigerated transportation, and mild refrigeration in stores, store-bought sprouts can have salmonella. You are better off growing your sprouts at home. There you can watch every stage, taste them often, and monitor their freshness. Start by adding them to some of the meals you make. This step alone will provide added nutrition and enzymes to any cooked, enzyme-deficient meal.

Sprouts are wonderful when added to your favorite sandwich. There are many kinds of breads that you can use. Sprouted yeast breads are light and fluffy like the breads that are traditionally eaten. Sprouted Manna breads are simply ground-up wheat sprouts that are cooked at lower temperatures; they contain no yeast, and they are dense and moist and usually eaten as open-faced sandwiches. There are sprouted wheat tortillas, pita pocket breads, and all sorts of breads made with flours. But one of the healthiest breads for your body's system is the Manna bread that you can make in your own kitchens from your own sprouted grains (see Chapter 8). Whatever type of bread you choose, remember: sprouts balance out acidity that the yeast breads create. You can make a healthy sandwich and pack it full of vegetables, avocados and sprouts, and season them with any of the dressings in Chapter 13. You will *love* these sandwiches.

Most of us have spent a lot of money and time making sure we store plenty of grains, seeds and beans for a rainy day. So why wait? Let's start using what we have on hand and integrate these super foods into our day-to-day life. As we rotate and use older grains, seeds and nuts, we bring added life to our meals.

Bring these foods you have stored to life, and bring life to your cells—today!

~Recipes~

Fast Sprouted Pocket Sandwiches
Open 1- whole wheat pita bread (or any bread you like).
Smear the sides with your favorite mustard and/or Veganaise (available in the fridge section of the Health Food Store).
Fill pocket with lentil sprouts or other sprouts.
Add 1 sliced tomato (optional).
Avocado slices (optional).
Sprinkle with "Spike Seasoning" and use one of "Vicki's Dressings".
Eat with a large "greens" salad.
Enjoy with a napkin!

Vegan Potato Salad with Sprouts
Baking potatoes, baked, cooled and chopped, with the *skins on.*

Add:

1 small onion, chopped (optional)

7-8 sweet or dill pickles, chopped (or ½ C sweet relish)

Moisten with Veganaise.

Favorite Mustard (to taste)

1-2 cup of favorite sprouts, such as: lentils, garbanzo beans, peas, mung beans, etc.

Season with "Real Salt" and pepper (to taste).

Mix and let sit in refrigerator to season.

Serve over a bed of alfalfa sprouts and a large 'greens' salad.

4-Bean Salad (Cooked Version)

2 cans each green beans, yellow wax beans, garbanzo beans, and kidney beans (you can fresh cook the green and yellow beans if you like, use about 2 cups each fresh beans).

> 1 large red onion, sliced
>
> 1 green pepper and 1 red pepper, sliced thin (optional)
>
> 2 cups sprouted lentils, peas, garbanzo beans, adzuki beans, mung beans, etc.

Marinade Sauce:

> 1 cup cold pressed oil
>
> ¾ cup raw apple cider vinegar
>
> ¾ cup raw honey
>
> Spike, "Real Salt" and pepper (to taste)

Marinate 8 hours in the fridge.

Sprouted Bean Salad (Raw Version)
Follow marinade sauce recipe for 4 Bean Salad.
Add:

> Sprouted green and red lentils, garbanzo beans,
> sprouted or fresh peas, adzuki beans, mung beans,
> etc.
>
> 2 cups each of fresh *raw uncooked* green beans and
> yellow wax beans, thinly French-cut sliced
>
> 1 red onion, thinly sliced
>
> 1 red and green pepper, thinly sliced

Mix. Marinate for at least 3 hours. This recipe can also
be made with the sprouted beans and the Marinade
Sauce without the veggies.

Remember, marinating breaks down foods to
either tenderize them or blend in the flavors.
Marinated salads will only last 2-3 days before the vinegar starts to break them down. Try to manage your
leftovers so that you eat them within 2-3 days.
Remember to always eat these marinated salads over a
big bed of greens for ultimate nutrition (see Chapter
13).

Creamy French Sprouted Dressing
In blender add:

> 1 cup of cold pressed oil
>
> ½ cup of apple cider vinegar
>
> ¼ cup of Kikkoman Soy Sauce or Nama Shoyu (raw
> soy sauce)

A 6-second squirt of ketchup

A 2-second squirt of mustard

2 Tbsp. raw honey

3 stalks celery

½ red Pepper

¼ small onion

1 sprig Rosemary (optional)

1 clove fresh garlic

1-2 cups red lentil sprouts

Juice of 1 lemon

Blend until smooth. Keeps in the fridge for about a week.

You can add any kind of sprout to this recipe. Because the sprouts are full of assimilable protein, this particular dressing is more protein-packed than others in this book. Weight lifters, athletes, pregnant or nursing mothers, children, and older persons will find this dressing satisfying as well as sufficient for protein requirements. It is delicious with Lemon Tahini Dressing (see Chapter 13). Mixing and matching flavors is what brings variety and passion to salad meals.

BRING YOUR FOOD **ALIVE!**
SPROUTS ARE
LIFE-GENERATING
FOOD.

Chapter 6

How Do I Use All of These Sprouts?

Once you begin sprouting, you'll discover that it is easy and fun! You may find yourself wanting to purchase more trays, and learn how to use sprouts in salads and other delicious dishes. Use your creativity and be daring as you add sprouts to your daily meals.

Begin by tasting them in their trays. You'll be amazed by how good they are. If you have children, let them help you grow and sample them. Next, add sprouts to your salads. Remember to eat a salad *first* before eating anything else at lunch and dinner. Eat a 'living food' *before* you eat a snack, cookie, candy, or something that may not be very healthy. You want living enzymes to get into your mouth first so your brain can define them and send a message to your body that there are sufficient enzymes to digest this meal. Every time you eat something, your body thinks that it is a meal. In addition to your salad at lunch you may want to substitute sprouts for some of the high fatty, over-processed foods that you are used to, or at least add the sprouts to them.

Pocket bread sandwiches (see Chapter 5) are popular. So are the veggie burrito wraps made with the sprouted wheat tortillas that you can buy in the refrigerated section of health food stores. And you'll love the Manna Stack Open-faced Sandwich made with Manna Bread from the freezer section of health food stores. These breads aren't considered *living-raw foods*, but as you *transition* to eating more living foods, these items are delicious and act as a base to help you include more sprouts and raw foods into your diet. The dressings in Chapter 13 provide added flavors and textures that you can't duplicate in a restaurant or at a fast food place.

Let your creativity soar by adding sprouts to any uncooked dish. Marinated salads are great when sprouts are added (see Chapter 13). They are crunchy and their texture is interesting to the palate. Because sprouts are a raw food, you should try to avoid killing their enzymes by cooking them. To improve texture and nutrition to your normal meals, add sprouts as a condiment on the side or to a cooked dish. Add your sprouts to dressings; make gourmet pâtés; make crackers and breads and even cookies! You can use sprouts in your food dehydrator then eat them as crunchy snacks and as healthy croutons for your salads. This book is full of recipes and ideas to get you started. Try these recipes, and then adjust them to fit your own unique taste.

Crackers and Croutons

Any sprout can be used to create your own crackers that you can season to fit *your* taste buds and the taste buds of your family. Decide which tastes that you like, search for seasonings or sauces that match that flavor then add sprouts and sprouted dishes. If the sauces aren't so healthy at first, don't worry—your immediate goal is just to get the good stuff down. Later on, as you taste buds adjust, you will begin to use healthier ingredients for seasoning to create delicious tastes. You *can* and *will* enjoy the flavors of healthier foods.

For a healthy substitute for Corn Nut-type snacks, simply shake lentil sprouts or soaked almonds in a covered container or bag with any healthy seasoning, such as Cajun, Mexican, Indian Curry, or Chinese Tamari. Then spread the seasoned sprouts on the mesh tray in your dehydrator. Set at 105° F until the sprouts are crisp. These are yummy, crunchy, healthy snacks that you can substitute for greasy chips and those deep-fried snacks.

Sprouted crackers are a favorite with any salad, with a dip or just eaten alone. They are particularly good when you dip them into a fresh guacamole or the Lemon Tahini Dip or dressing. Use them instead of potato chips with your sandwiches...the possibilities are endless!

Don't waste your raw-food leftovers. Throw them into the blender with some fresh sprouts, add seasonings to fit your taste, and then dehydrate them until they are crisp. These random "left-over" crackers are sometimes the best. Remember, when you dehydrate the cracker batter, it becomes more flavorful as it is dehydrated. The flavors become concentrated, so be sure not to spice or salt it too much before you turn out the batter onto the solid dehydrator sheets. You don't want the crackers to be too salty or over-flavored. It is safer to *under-flavor* the batter when it is in the blender. Some of my best cracker recipes were inspired from raw food leftovers!

Store your crisp crackers and croutons in air-tight containers and keep them in a cool, dry spot. If they become soft, just put them back in the dehydrator. If you are storing them for a long time, place a paper towel in the airtight bags to absorb any extra moisture. As long as no moisture gets inside, they will store indefinitely.

Here's another dehydrating tip: soaked and sprouted almonds and nuts are great when they are dehydrated until they are crisp. You can eat them later as a snack, or you can add them into a healthy trail-mix. The fresh, soaked nuts only last 3-4 days in the fridge. Dehydrating them is an easy and fun way to have sprouted foods on hand, which you can grab when you are running out the door! Be sure that you are eating any dehydrated food with your greens or salads, and that you drink plenty of water each day. Remember that these foods are dehydrated and will immediately absorb moisture when they are exposed to it. Even the moisture in your body will re-hydrate dehydrated crackers as you eat them. By keeping up on your *drink-a-gallon-of-pure-water-everyday* routine, you help your body from becoming water-depleted, which can lead to constipation (a possibility caused by eating too many dehydrated foods alone or without water-rich foods to counter balance them).

Sunflower and Lentil Croutons

1 cup soaked sunflower seeds, rinsed

1 cup lentil sprouts, rinsed

Pour into a zipper-lock bag ¼ cup of dry chili seasoning. Place sprouts (½ cup at a time) in the bag. Zip it
locked and shake until coated. Lay out contents on
dehydrator at 105° F until crisp. Serve as croutons or a
snack.

Sun-Dried Tomato Chips

In a blender add:

> ½ cup wheat sprouts
>
> ¼ cup lentil sprouts
>
> 3 sprigs of parsley
>
> 3 sprigs of cilantro
>
> 1 sprig of fresh basil
>
> ½ bell pepper
>
> ½ Anaheim pepper
>
> ½ small onion
>
> 1 clove garlic
>
> 2 tsp. cumin
>
> 1 tsp. chili powder
>
> 3-4 Tbsp. Nama Shoyu or Kikkoman
>
> "Real Salt" and pepper, to taste

Blend well.

Turn blender off.

Add:

    2 large tomatoes, chopped

    Pulse 3-5 times so that they are still chunky.

    Fold out on dehydrator sheets.

    Dehydrate at 105° F for 1-2 days.

Flax Crackers

Soak 3 cups flax seeds overnight in a blender

Coarsely blend:

    Juice of one orange

    3 stalks celery, chopped

    1 red onion, chopped

    2 cloves garlic

    Handful of fresh basil, cilantro & parsley

    3 tsp. chili powder

    3 tsp. cumin

    3 tsp. Nama shoyu, or Kikkoman Soy sauce

Add 3 small tomatoes, chopped.

Blend coarsely to keep tomatoes chunky. Pulse 2-3 times.

Stir in soaked flax seeds.

Pour out batter on solid dehydrator sheets.

Dehydrate at 105 degrees for about 4-6 hours.

Turn tray over and peel off cracker to dehydrate on other side for another 4-8 hours until crisp.

Sprouted wheat and grain

Sprouted wheat is one of the best ways to get pure antioxidants into the body. Wheat sprouts are ready in the tray in about 24-48 hours. The tail should be visible when you start to use the sprout; don't let the tail get much longer than the size of the grain (see Chapter 11).

Natural Antioxidant

Whenever the body sustains an injury, disease, trauma, or even reacts to daily workouts, the body emits free radicals that must be scavenged by antioxidants to prevent damage. For example, you sometimes can feel your muscles become sore after a heavy workout. This is lactic-acid buildup in your muscles and joints. By using wheatgrass juice after a workout and eating something full of wheat sprouts, you can help integrate antioxidants that literally eat up and remove free radials. Recipes for sprouted wheat crackers and breads and even cookies are scattered throughout this book. The recipes are delicious ways to get your daily dose of antioxidants...without taking a pill!

With just a little planning, you can spend only ten minutes a day—or 30-60 minutes a few times each week—to make some delicious foods that you can add to your salads and dips—a much wiser choice than indulging in processed foods and a lot cheaper than buying these foods in a store. Just for fun, substitute wheat sprouts for a plate of pasta and add your favorite spaghetti sauce. You will still have the chewy texture that you're used to, and you won't have the *fast sugar* addiction to the pasta or that *heavy* feeling that comes from eating foods made with flour.

Sprouted Spaghetti

    1-2 C wheat sprouts

    Spaghetti Sauce of your choice.

Vicki's Favorite Spaghetti Sauce (cooked)

In a crockpot, add:

    2-16 oz. cans stewed tomatoes (blended if you don't like chunks)

    1 can stewed tomatoes, unblended

    2 cans tomato paste

    4 Tbsp. dried basil (or 2 large bunches fresh basil, chopped)

Simmer in an open crockpot all day.

Raw Soups

These soups are surprisingly good and a great raw food for the elderly or infants who may be struggling with their teeth. But regardless of how good these soups are, don't let them substitute for a big plate of salad greens. Eat them with your 'greens' salads.

Raw Corn Chowder

Blend: (straining is optional)

   1-2 cups of almonds, soaked

   4 cups of water

Add:

   6 fresh ears cob corn

   1/8 large onion

   1 cup of carrot juice

   3 tomatillos (optional) or 1 Tbsp. lemon juice

   1-2 avocados (for desired thickness)

   2-3 tsp. cumin

   2-3 tsp. kelp, Spike or "Real Salt" and pepper (to taste)

Blend until smooth.

Serve cold.

Raw Butternut Soup

In a blender, add:

   1 cup butternut squash, chopped, peeled and seeded

   ½ cup soaked almonds

   1 cup soaked sesame seeds

   4 green onions, chopped

   ¼ cup jicama, chopped

   ½ red pepper

   Rejuvelac or water to turn the blades (for desired thickness)

Season with:

   2-3 tsp. coriander

2-3 Tbsp. Nama Shoyu or Kikkoman

1 sprig fresh mint leaves (optional)

Kelp powder, "Spike" or "Real Salt" (to taste)

Blend until smooth.

Serve with fresh mint sprig.

Pâté

A pâté is a paste made of blended sprouts and vegetables. This is definitely a gourmet raw food. Because these foods are so concentrated and full of nuts and seeds, make sure that you are eating a large plate of greens before or with the pâté. The pâté is so good that you may find yourself indulging in it. You may want to curb your temptation to indulge so you won't experience bloating and gas. Use a Champion Juicer-type of homogenizer or try in *your* blender or a Vita Mix high-speed blender.

Island Almond Loaf Pâté

Juice 1 cup of carrot juice

Run simultaneously through your Champion Juicer using the blank:

2 med. carrots peeled

2 cups of soaked almonds (soaked for 48 hrs.)

This will make a thick pâté.

Add to almond pâté mixture:

1 cup of finely chopped celery

2 cup of chopped green onions

1 cup of seed cheese (optional for protein)

2 tsp. kelp

3 tsp. curry (or to taste)

"Real Salt" (optional)

Mix all ingredients together.

Use ¼ cup of carrot juice while mixing to soften the dough if necessary.

Mix well (forms a dough).

Serve as a loaf or individually inside lettuce leafs.

Top with sunflower curry dip.

Enjoy!

Sunflower Curry Dip or Sauce

¾ cups of soaked sunflower seeds

1cup of carrot juice

1-3 tsp. curry powder

Dash of Spike

Blend, using Rejuvelac for desired consistency.

(Add more sunflower seeds to thicken.)

Serve as a dip or a sauce.

Enjoy!

Legumes and Lentils

Legumes include all the bean family. If you are an athlete, you will crave these foods. If you eat a lot of legumes, you have to *work* your body to use up the extra protein. Exercise everyday to use the abundance of proteins that are in rich supply in legumes. Make sure you are eating a plate of greens before you eat these foods; you can experience some uncomfortable bloating if you eat too much.

Lentil seed balls or burgers

Mince:

    ½ green and red pepper

    3 celery stalks

    1 bunch green onions

    8 mushrooms (optional)

    ½ bunch of fresh parsley

    1 sprig of fresh basil or 2 Tbsp. of dried basil

    3 cloves of fresh garlic

    2 cups of green lentil sprouts (with small tails)

Finely shred:

    3 small zucchini

    ½ butternut squash

Grind in blender:

    2 cups of soaked sunflower seeds

    1 cup of soaked sesame seeds

    2 Tbsp. dried or fresh basil

    1 Tbsp. of caraway or dill seed

Mix together and season with:

    ¼ cup Nama Shoyu or Kikkoman

    Spike, Kelp or "Real Salt" (to taste)

    Fresh ground pepper and Spike (to taste)

Form into balls and dehydrate at 105° F until firm, but not hard (about 6 hours until an outside crust is formed).

(If you have a Champion Juicer, you can run the seeds and squash through it.)

Serve on a bed of alfalfa sprouts, lentil sprouts, or fenugreek sprouts with a large salad of greens.

Top with the Sunflower Curry Dip or Sweet Red Pepper Sauce.

Sweet Red Pepper Sauce

In a blender add:

> 1 cup of soaked sunflower seeds
> ½ red pepper
> ¼ - ½ red onion
> 2 cloves garlic
> 1-2 tsp. cumin (optional)
> 1 Tbsp. Spike (to taste)
> ¼ tsp. Mexican seasoning
> "Real Salt" and pepper (to taste)

Blend well and use as a dip or dressing.

Burgers

Instead of rolling the pâtés into balls, pat them into patties. Dehydrate them to be crusty on the outside and softer on the inside, and use them in the first three days. Afterwards, place them back in the dehydrator and dehydrate all of the moisture out of them. Store them in airtight bags with a paper towel. Great for a quick treat, with your salad, or for camping and back-packing.

Create your own dish by using a dressing or sauce over top of them, or to fill out a dinner alongside your greens salad. Use Manna Bread as the bun and dress up your burger just like you would a traditional one. Enjoy!

Raw Veggie Bean Burgers

Juice any vegetable juice (with screen).

Save the pulp.

Run through the Champion (with blank) 1 cup each:

    Garbanzo bean sprouts

    Lentil sprouts

    Adzuki sprouts

    Whole peas

(Use a carrot simultaneously to push sprouts through.)

This makes a pâté.

Add together in a separate bowl:

    1 bunch green onions, chopped

    2 cups carrot juice pulp

    1 red pepper, chopped

    1 tsp. cumin

    2 tsp. "Real Salt" or Spike (to taste)

    1 Tbsp. basil

    1 tsp. fresh or dried rosemary

    3 Tbsp. Nama Shoyu or Kikkoman

3 Tbsp. vegetarian Worcestershire Sauce (optional)

Knead.

Form into patties ½" thick and place on oiled dehydrator screen.

Dehydrate at 105° F for 2 hours.

Turn, dehydrate 1 hour more, until outside is crusty and inside is soft.

Serve alone or with Manna bread slices with fry sauce, ketchup, mustard, lettuce, pickles, tomatoes, etc.!

Get creative!

Almond Burgers

Alternate through Champion blender with the blank:

> 1 cup soaked almonds
>
> 2 carrots
>
> ½ cup each sprouted lentils and garbanzo beans
>
> ½ cup sprouted wheat

Finely chop:

> 5 stalks celery
>
> 2 bunches green onion

Mix together and season with:

> ¼ cup Nama Shoyu
>
> 1 tsp. Spike
>
> 4 tsp. curry
>
> "Real Salt" and pepper (to taste)

Form into patties.

Dehydrate at 105° F for 6 hours, turn and dehydrate 1-2 hours more.

Fry Sauce

½ cup Veganaise (fridge section of the Health Food Store)

1/3 cup ketchup of your choice (to taste)

Mix together.

Use for: Dipping raw veggies

Dipping steamed veggies

A great sauce for burgers

A dip for the raw crackers

Note: Fry Sauce is a transitional food, not a raw food. As you are getting used to the tastes and textures of raw greens and sprouts, you may find this helpful.

Refried Beans

Here is a mock refried beans recipe that is made of soaked sunflower seeds. If you play with the cumin and the Mexican herbs, you can match the texture and flavor of really good refried beans...except they won't be cooked! Here is an example of how you can create an entire meal around a sprouted food...Mexican style!

Raw Refried Beans

2 cups soaked sunflower seeds

¼ small onion

1 small tomato

1-3 tsp. cumin

3 tsp. Nama Shoyu, or Kikkoman

½ tsp. "Real Salt" or Spike (to taste)

3 Tbsp. Mexican herbs (to taste) and a slice of
jalapeno is optional!

Blend, using Rejuvelac to help turn the blades for
desired consistency.

Pico de Gallo Salsa

Dice:

> 3-4 ripe tomatoes
>
> 1 bunch green onions
>
> 1 fresh jalapeño (or part of it, seeds are optional!)
>
> 1 handful cilantro
>
> 1 clove garlic (pressed)
>
> Fresh lime juice

Mix together and serve!

You can use this as a great dressing.

This is great as a salsa for your dehydrated chips, and a
much healthier choice than eating deep-fried tortilla
chips, which are really hard on the gall bladder.

Raw Tacos Mexican Style

Scoop raw refried beans (see above recipe) into lettuce
boats.

Add:

> Grated carrots, cabbage, celery, red pepper, etc.
>
> Chopped sunflower greens, kale, lettuces
>
> Guacamole and Pico de Gallo
>
> Roll, eat and enjoy!

Mock Tofu

Sprouted foods can be creative substitutes for the over-processed soybean in tofu. This "tofu" is made with soaked pine nuts and sunflower seeds. Roll these up in a lettuce leaf and you will have a delicious meal Chinese style!

Raw Sunflower Garlic Tofu

½ cup soaked pine nuts

2 cups soaked sunflower seeds

1 clove garlic

¼ small onion

3 sprigs fresh parsley

1 tsp expeller pressed sesame oil (optional)

Fresh orange juice to turn the blades.

In a separate bowl, add:

1 cup finely chopped celery

1 cup finely minced green onions

Mix together and let sit about an hour to mix the flavors.

Use as the filling for Chinese tacos, as a dip, or as a thick dressing.

Chinese Tacos

Fill a lettuce leaf with:

Sunflower garlic tofu

Grated cabbage, carrot and parsnip

Raw sweet and sour sauce

Enjoy!

Raw Sweet and Sour Sauce

½ cup soaked pitted dates blended with:

2 tsp. brown rice vinegar or apple cider vinegar

4 Tbsp. olive oil

3 tsp. Nama Shoyu or Kikkoman (to taste)

4 tsp. mustard (hot mustard is optional)

2 inches of fresh ginger, pressed

1 Umeboshi plum (optional)

¾ cup fresh orange juice

¼ cup fresh lemon juice

4-6 soaked-pitted dates, pure maple syrup or raw honey (to taste)

Blend well. You can add fresh pineapple juice too, if desired.

This is good as a salad dressing too.

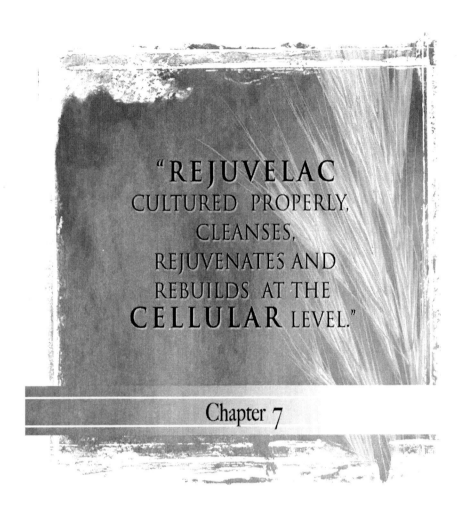

"REJUVELAC
CULTURED PROPERLY,
CLEANSES,
REJUVENATES AND
REBUILDS AT THE
CELLULAR LEVEL."

Chapter 7

Live Fermented Foods

Fermented foods are high in assimilable proteins and B vitamins. They contain carbohydrates and are packed with enzymes. As we have learned, enzymes assist in breaking down large molecules of food into smaller, assimilable units that can be carried through the bloodstream to feed the body. But all enzymes aren't created equal. Because enzymes also break down deposits of aggregated or stored sugars, fats and proteins, which the body can't break down on its own, enzymes *must be fresh* to be powerful enough to get to the blocked areas of the bowels and to do the job right.

Raw, lactose-free live bacteria surpass any bottled enzymes, acidophilus or bifidis that you might purchase at a store. Live bacteria work together *with* enzymes to break down aggregated blockages and quickly remove them from the body. Fermented foods are naturally predigested, having broken down proteins into amino acids, and having broken down carbohydrates into simple sugars. Fermented food replenishes enzymes for better digestion and cleansing of the body. Fermented foods remove toxic waste so toxins cannot be absorbed through the colon wall into the bloodstream to be recycled again.

Rejuvelac

Rejuvelac is the fermented liquid of sprouted wheat in its concentrated form. It is a healthy drink that literally brings rejuvenation to the body. Digestion is greatly improved by drinking one quart of Rejuvelac each day.

Rejuvelac and Seed Cheese (recipe in the following chapter) contain lactic acid, which destroys the harmful bacteria in the intestines, and reduces lactic acid buildup in the muscles when you exercise.

Rejuvelac is a natural acidophilus that fortifies the friendly bacteria in the colon and small intestines.

Rejuvelac is one of the most valuable foods that will cleanse and rebuild the intestinal tract—from the mouth all the way down through the colon.

As a rule, do not purchase any imitation Rejuvelac brands in stores for the same reason that you should not purchase sprouts in stores—neither item keeps well.

One batch of Rejuvelac will last about three days if you drink one quart a day. You can either drink it all at once or throughout the day.

Rejuvelac gives you energy. It contains carbohydrates and is a perfect food. If you are on the juice phase of cleansing, you will find Rejuvelac to be satisfying and energy-producing. Athletes often use Rejuvelac in the place of salty electrolyte drinks to replace valuable carbohydrates, minerals and electrolytes, or to stabilize their sugar levels for more endurance with little to no let down time.

Drinking Rejuvelac everyday also helps curb sugar cravings. This is valuable to people who are concerned with weight loss or who struggle to make healthier choices in their daily diets. Rejuvelac helps you get through those uncomfortable times when you are changing your lifestyle to a healthier one.

How to Make Rejuvelac

You will need three glass quart jars, one gallon glass jar (like a Sun Tea Jar or a pickle jar from the deli), a blender, some cheesecloth, a thick rubber band, and a large, *pourable* bowl or pitcher.

1. Soak 2 cups soft white wheat in a glass quart jar for 8-12 hours or overnight. Pour into sprouting trays and rinse well. Sprout in trays 12-36 hours, rinsing and draining every morning and every evening.
2. Place sprouts in the blender with 1 quart steamed distilled water. Blend for 10 seconds, just to break up the grain.
3. Pour into a 1-gallon glass jar, and fill to the top with water. Cover with cheesecloth and a rubber band.
4. Let it sit on the counter (68°-80°) for 6-24 hours until it becomes slightly sour smelling like unsweetened lemonade.
5. Pour through a seed bag or cheesecloth, straining it into a large bowl. Pour from the bowl into 3 glass quart jars. Discard the remaining blended wheat.
6. Cover lightly with a lid and refrigerate for 3-4 days. Drink one quart each day. Rejuvelac should taste slightly sour like unsweetened lemonade. It may *smell* spoiled and still be okay. If it *tastes* spoiled, it probably is. Throw it away and start over.

The longer you leave the Rejuvelac to ferment the more enzymes are created. Sometimes Rejuvelac may become slightly carbonated. The flavor is usually strong at this point. The carbonation indicates that the enzymes are very strong; you may find that you can only drink a pint of this kind. Find the taste and texture that works best for you. The longer you drink the Rejuvelac the more you may find that you like the stronger flavor and enzymes.

Start by using the soft white wheat, if you have a choice. This wheat has a sweet flavor and is easiest to get used to, although any grain will work. Each grain has its own unique flavor. For example, rye and hard winter wheat have a little stronger taste; un-hulled barley and whole un-hulled oats have a little starchier flavor. You can use amaranth grain, spelt, quinoa grain, or any grain that grows indigenous in your area. Experiment for different varieties and flavors.

Practice, practice, practice! For the sake of your body, the effort is worth the reward. Remember, every time you pour off the finished Rejuvelac into the 3 glass quart jars, start soaking another two cups of wheat to grow for your next batch.

If at first you are struggling with the taste of the Rejuvelac, try to drink it alone *followed* with some juice. But if you can swallow it alone, it will quickly be assimilated into your system without its being diluted. As with wheatgrass juice, do whatever you can to get

Rejuvelac into your body everyday. As your body
cleanses out the addictive foods and flavorings, your
taste buds will adapt.

Rejuvelac Sun Crackers

Sun crackers are the dehydrated form of
Rejuvelac and sprouted wheat—the pinnacle of concentrated nutrition! As these crackers are dehydrated at
105° F, their enzymes, vitamins, acidophilus, proteins
and carbohydrates are preserved and locked into a concentrated form that maximizes their optimum nutrition
and assimilation. They are great eaten along with a
salad, with a dip, as an open-face tostada, with
Sprouted Refried Beans, sprouts, avocado and Spike, or
as a chip for salsa and guacamole—this is the basic
recipe. To it you can add whatever leftover veggies you
have on hand and season everything to suit your taste!

Sun Crackers
Fill blender ½ full of sprouted wheat.
Add same amount of Rejuvelac or water.
*Note: water makes the cracker tougher; Rejuvelac makes
the cracker more delicate.*
Blend to pancake-batter consistency.
Pour on solid dehydrator sheets. Dehydrate at 105° F
until crisp.
This basic recipe is rather tasteless, so you may want to
add any combination of:

Spike

"Real Salt" and pepper

Parsley

Basil

Oregano

¼ red onion

Garlic

And any herbs or seasonings that compliment your veggies.

Spicy Rye Garlic Crackers

2 cups rye sprouts

1 stalk celery

1 clove garlic

¼ small red onion

1 Anaheim pepper

½ green pepper

Season to taste with the following:

Nama Shoyu or Kikkoman Soy sauce

"Real Salt" or Spike, if needed

Italian seasonings (to taste)

Add Rejuvelac to help turn the blender blades.

Blend until the contents become a coarsely ground batter.

Dehydrate at 105° F degrees for 1-2 days, until crisp.

Garlic Sun Crackers

Fill blender ½ full of sprouted wheat and quinoa in equal proportions.

Add:

> 5 cloves garlic
>
> Spike to taste

When blending, add enough Rejuvelac to make a pancake-batter consistency.

Pour onto solid dehydrator sheets.

Dehydrate at 105° F, until crisp.

Rejuvelac-Avocado-Dill Dip

Blend:

> 3 avocados
>
> ¼ small onion
>
> 2-3 cloves fresh garlic
>
> 2 tomatillos (optional)
>
> ¼ cucumber (optional)
>
> Juice of 1 lime or lemon
>
> ½ tsp. dill seed

Add Rejuvelac to desired consistency.

Blend until smooth.

Use as a dip for Sun Crackers.

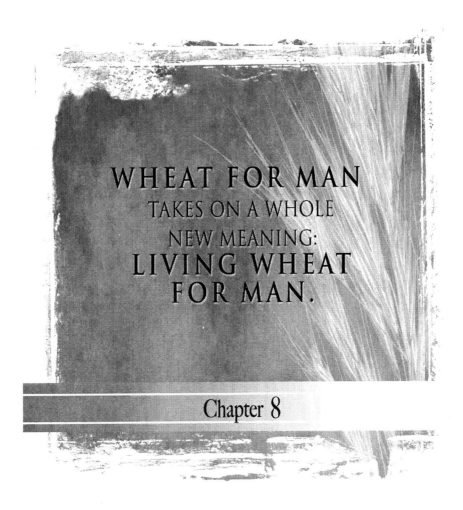

WHEAT FOR MAN
TAKES ON A WHOLE
NEW MEANING:
LIVING WHEAT
FOR MAN.

Chapter 8

Sprouted Grains, Breads, Cookies and Cereals

Sprouted Breads

Sprouted breads are wonderful additions to any raw meal. Many athletes depend on sprouted grains for proper carbohydrate intake and balanced proteins. The common denominator of *all* sprouted breads is that they aren't cooked and they don't contain yeast. The nutrients in sprouted breads are higher in quality than their cooked-bread counterparts.

As you see in the bread and pâté recipes, you are instructed to run the sprouts through your Champion Juicer simultaneously with carrots, onions, celery, etc. to prevent the machine from seizing up from the density of the sprouts (for information on the Champion Juicer see Chapter 14). To achieve the desired dough consistency, use as many or as few vegetables as you wish. Then after adding the other ingredients, knead the dough to meld the flavors and create the desired consistency. While your hands are wet, form the dough into patties about the size of a slice of store bought Manna Bread and set the patties on the mesh trays of the dehydrator. Don't worry about getting the edges too close together —this bread doesn't rise!

Dehydrate at 105° F for about four hours. Turn over the whole mesh tray with the bread on the other side, and then dehydrate the other side of the bread for another 3-4 hours. When the bread is crusty on the outside and soft on the inside, it is ready to use. This is a perfect addition to your *living-food* dinner; your *concentrated-food* dinner with a huge greens salad, or an open-faced sandwich. Or you may want to just enjoy it plain! At this stage, you can store it in the refrigerator and it will last between 3-4 days. After that, to prevent spoiling, you will need to put the remainder back in the dehydrator until you remove all the moisture. Store in airtight storage bags with a paper towel in it to absorb any other moisture.

In the stores, Manna Bread is sold in loaves. Look carefully and you will see that the bread has been baked above 105° F; the crust on the bottom of the bread will be thick. The higher temperature has created a bread-like texture inside the thick loaf. This is a telltale sign of cooked Manna Bread as opposed to raw Manna Bread.

I form my bread into *slices* to dehydrate, and I use it as if it were bread already sliced! Otherwise, if you prefer a loaf to a slice of raw Manna Bread, you run the risk of the middle of the loaf prematurely fermenting.

For convenience and to accommodate a busy lifestyle, make these crackers, breads, and cookies ahead of time. Add them to fresh salads or use them for raw foods on the go! When I travel, I always take a couple of airtight plastic bags filled with fully dehydrated breads, burgers and crackers. In that way, I can add nutritious raw food to anything I eat.

Simple Raw Essene Bread
Run through the Champion Juicer, with a *blank*:
> 2 cups of sprouted wheat and 2 stalks of celery (run through simultaneously)

This will make dough.

Add:

   1 tsp. dill seed

   1 sprig dill weed leaves

   ½ tsp. "Real Salt" or Spike (to taste)

Using wet hands, form into slices, about ½" thick.

Place in food dehydrator: 4 hours on one side then 4 hours on the other side.

Options:

   In place of a food processor, you can use a meat grinder or grinder-type juicer on the meat grinding setting.

   You can flavor with anything! Use juice pulp and herbs for vegetable bread, or you can use fruit for nut bread.

Hearty Protein Bread Slices

Juice any vegetable juice (use screen on Champion Juicer) and save the pulp.

Run through Champion Juicer, with *blank*:

   Soaked sunflower seeds, sesame seeds,

   sprouted wheat, lentils, soaked almonds, etc.

   Use onion, celery and carrot simultaneously to prevent the machine from seizing.

Mix with juice pulp.

Add caraway seeds (optional).

Season to taste with Spike, Nama Shoyu, and natural seasoning herbs.

Spread on solid dehydrator trays and score into squares, or shape them into patties with wet hands.

Dehydrate on 105° F for six hours, then turn and dehydrate for 3-6 hours more.

Hearty Wheat Manna Bread Slices

Run through Champion Juicer, with *blank*:

  4 cups sprouted wheat

  5 carrots

  ¼ large onion

Run simultaneous to make dough.

Add:

  1 tsp. "Real Salt"

  1 tsp. Spike

  1 tsp. Italian seasoning

  1 tsp. dill seed

  1 tsp. Nama Shoyu raw soy sauce

  2-4 Tbsp. date powder or raw honey

Shape into ¼" patties. Place on screen dehydrator trays. Dehydrate at 105° F for 3-4 hours. Turn and dehydrate 3-4 hours more or until desired consistency.

Power Manna Bread

In your Champion Juicer, save the pulp from juicing:

  8 carrots

  3 beets (you can use the pulp from your juice cleanse)

  1 bunch celery

In the Champion Juicer with the blank, make a dough:

   1 cup soaked amaranyth seeds

   1 cup soaked hulled pumpkin seeds

   2 cup soaked quinoa seeds

   2 cup soaked sunflower seeds

Alternating with:

   4-6 cloves garlic, peeled

   ½ small onion, chopped

Mix together with:

   3 tsp. honey

   6 tsp. Nama Shoyu

   1 tsp. kelp powder

   2 tsp. cumin powder

   3 tsp. curry powder

   1/3 cup brown flax seeds (un-soaked)

Form into patties.

Dehydrate at 105° F for 3 hour; turn,

Dehydrate for 3 more hours until crisp on outside
and still moist on the inside.

Manna Stack Sandwich-Opened Faced

1-2 slices Manna Bread (purchase at health food store—
freezer section)

Or make your own!

Layer with:

   Veganaise (optional)

   Stone-ground mustard

   Sliced avocados

Bubbies Sauerkraut (optional)
Bubbies Bread and Butter pickles
Sliced tomatoes
Sprouts
Handful of "greens" salad
Any of Vicki's dressings. Yum!

Living Cereal

Are you still craving cereal and milk in the morning? This cereal will give you enough energy to last you past lunchtime! This cereal is very high in antioxidants, and with almond milk and dates, it provides a complete protein meal for athletes and busy adults. Be creative with what you add. Personally, I like to sprout the wheat for about 24 hours so it is soft, but not with too long a tail. Flax cereal is rich in complete Omega 3 nutrients, and it assists the bowels to move daily!

Sprouted Wheat Cereal (or Yummy Dessert!)

1 cup of wheat sprouts
Soaked sunflower seeds or any other soaked seeds, or nuts such as almonds, Brazil nuts, etc.
Dates, chopped
Raisins, currants, dehydrated cranberries, blueberries, apricots, etc.
½ cup of any combination of *fresh* fruit including:
Banana, chopped
Blueberries

Apple

Cherries

Apricots

Peach

Raspberries

Strawberries, etc.

Serve with almond milk.

Have fun!

Sprouted Almond Milk

Fill to top of blender blades with soaked almonds.

Add:

　　1 ½ - 2 cups of water

　　1-2 tsp. real vanilla

　　1 tsp real almond extract

　　2 tsp. real maple syrup, raw honey, or 3-5 soaked
　　and pitted dates

　　2 shakes of cinnamon (optional)

　　Ice cubes

Blend.

This is great on any kind of cereal.

The more water the thinner the milk; the less water the
thicker the cream.

Flax Cereal

In a small cereal bowl add:

　　1/3 cup flax seeds

A few teaspoons of sunflower seeds, sesame seeds, pumpkin seeds, etc.

A few soaked almonds, walnuts, pecans, filberts, etc.

¼ cup unsweetened coconut

¼ cup raisins, chopped dates, cranberries, etc.

3-4 Tbsp. date sugar, maple syrup or honey (to taste)

Raw carob powder (optional)

In the evening: Add a little more water than the seeds and cover the bowl.

In the morning: Stir the thickened cereal, adding more sweetener and vanilla, if desired, and add any fresh fruit. You can also stir in raw apple juice, or sprouted Almond Milk. Enjoy!

For 72-hour Kits: Use only dry ingredients and pack each single serving in a re-closable bag with a plastic spoon inside. All you have to do is add water the night before and the cereal will be thickened and ready to eat in the morning. Raisins and date sugar make the cereal sweet. Great for backpacking and campouts!

Cookies

Cookies are another wonderful way to utilize wheat sprouts. When I am training for a marathon or triathlon, I eat lots of these cookies, just like athletes eat power bars. Through your Champion Juicer, simultaneously blend fruits such as apples, pears or peaches with the wheat sprouts, so the machine doesn't seize up. Other fruit choices are raisins, dried cranberries, currents, dates and figs. These are carbohydrates that are easy to use and give consistent energy, unlike expensive "power" bars sold in stores. Sometimes I like the cookies soft, just like normal cookies, and sometimes I dehydrate them until there is no moisture so I can store them in airtight plastic bags with a paper towel inside. In this form, I can use them quickly, take them on the road, or plop them in my mouth as a snack with dates and bananas.

Almond Fortune Wafer
Run through the Champion juicer with the *blank:*
> 2 cups of soaked almonds
> Quartered peeled and chopped lemon

Add together in blender or Vita Mix with:
> ¼ cup shredded coconut
> 3 Tbsp. vanilla
> 1 lemon, juiced
> 2 tsp. almond flavoring
> 2 tsp. maple syrup or honey
> ¼ tsp. Coriander
> Orange juice to help blades turn

Blend to dough-like consistency.
Form into balls and flatten.
Dehydrate at 105° F for 1-2 hours then turn.
These are great to eat with fresh berry purée or with raw honey on top!

(If you don't have a Champion Juicer, throw it all in the blender and do your best!)

Apple Almond Cookies
Run simultaneously through Champion Juicer (with a blank) to make cookie dough:

> 2 cups white wheat sprouts (1 ½ days growth)
> 4 Fuji apples, quartered and seeded
> 1 cup of dates, soaked and pitted (soaked 4 hours)
> 2 cups of soaked almonds (soaked 48 hours)

Stir together in a bowl.
Add:

> 6 tsp. real vanilla
> 3-6 tsp. maple syrup or raw honey
> 1 tsp. cinnamon
> ½ tsp. nutmeg
> 2/3 cup of almonds or walnuts soaked, dehydrated, *and coarsely chopped*
> ¼ cup of date sugar (optional)
> ¼ cup of unsweetened coconut, finely grated (optional)
> ½ cup of raisins (optional)

Stir together and adjust to your taste.
Form into cookies on mesh dehydrator sheets about ½" thick.
Dehydrate at 105° F for 6-12 hours depending on the desired thickness of cookie.

Date, Almond & Apricot Cotlets—Raw

    1 cup of dates, dehydrated

    1 cup of apricots, dehydrated

    2 cup of almonds, soaked 48 hours (fresh or dehydrated)

Carefully place almonds through the center of the apricots and dates.

Arrange on a tray to snack on throughout the day.

These treats are great for hikes too!

Sesame Cream Macaroon Cookies

In a blender, blend:

    3 cups of soaked sesame seeds

    1 cup of soaked pine nuts

    2-3 cups of water

    6-8 soaked dates, pitted

Blend well, adding water to make a thick cream.

Add:

    Raw honey (to taste)

    2 tsp. real vanilla

    1 tsp. real almond extract

Pour into a bowl.

Add:

    2 cups of unsweetened coconut, shredded

    1 Tbsp. cinnamon (optional)

    ¼ tsp. nutmeg (optional)

    Pinch of "Real Salt"

    Enough almond milk to make cookie dough

Drop by teaspoon amounts to form balls.

Roll in coconut.

Place on dehydrator trays.

Dehydrate at 105° F for 3-4 hours until crisp on the outer shell.

Dip top of the cookie in raw honey and put back in the dehydrator for another 1-2 hours (optional).

Mmmmmm!

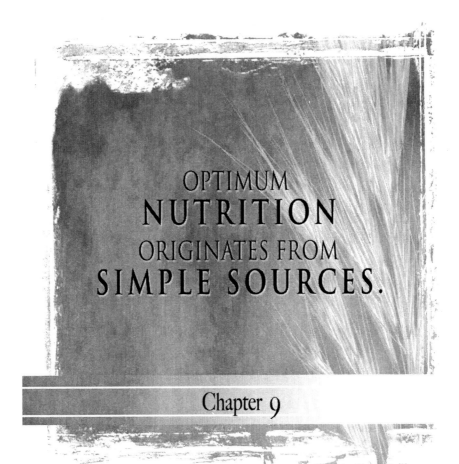

OPTIMUM
NUTRITION
ORIGINATES FROM
SIMPLE SOURCES.

Chapter 9

Soaking Seeds and Nuts

Growing seeds and nuts are a little different from sprouting grains and other legumes. The harvest time is sometimes faster, so they do not need time to sprout in the sprouting trays. Some of the seeds and nuts will sprout tails just like they do when they are grown in the sprouting trays. Almost overnight, most of the smaller seeds will sprout little tails. However, the nuts will usually not produce a tail to indicate they are sprouting; nevertheless they will swell almost twice their original size. Even though there may not be an outward sign of growth, much is happening under the skin.

When you soak the seed or nut for the first 8-10 hours, the phytic acid around the shell will begin to breakdown and dissolve. You will notice a dark residue on the bottom of the quart glass jar, which you should rinse thoroughly before refilling it with fresh water and allowing it to sit on the counter. At that time, some of the tiny seeds will be ready to harvest. If you are not going to use them immediately, let them drain on a paper towel, place them in an airtight bag, and keep them in the refrigerator until you are ready to use them. However, try to plan ahead so you can eat them fresh without refrigeration. Small seeds are time-sensitive and very fragile.

Make sure to soak the larger nuts for 48 hours. Change the water every morning and evening at the same time when you are watering your other sprouts. You should taste them constantly. The flavor and texture of the larger nuts is so much better...even after 24 hours.

Seed Cheese

Now that you are getting good at making Rejuvelac, you are ready to make the seed cheese. Rejuvelac is a major ingredient in seed cheese; it is the culture that starts the growth of the healthy bacteria. The chemical reaction of the natural proteins in the soaked sesame and sunflower seeds combined with the healthy bacteria from the Rejuvelac creates a perfect protein in the seed cheese.

How to make Seed Cheese:
1. Soak 1 cup of raw sunflower seeds and ½ cup of brown sesame seeds in a quart glass jar, and fill it to the top with water. Let it sit uncovered on the counter all day.
2. Drain in the evening. Put the soaked seeds in the blender with enough Rejuvelac to turn the blades. While the blades are spinning, add enough Rejuvelac to make a thick paste. Blend until smooth.
3. Pour the paste from the blender into a seed bag or wrap it in cheesecloth. Twist the bag tightly by attaching a twist-tie to squeeze out the watery whey. Hang it over your sink to drain at (68° - 80°) all night. (I use a rubber band to tie it to the water faucet and let it drain in the sink all night.)
4. In the morning, attach the seed bag to a fridge rack with a twist-tie, or if you have glass shelves, place a heavy bottle on the top of the cheesecloth and hang

the cheese ball from the rack underneath. Let it hang in the fridge with a bowl underneath to drain for 6-8 hours. Most of the draining will take place in the sink overnight, so the cheese ball will be pretty dry. When it is done, it will be harder, about the consistency of cream cheese.

5. Remove from the bag or cheesecloth. Place in an airtight, covered container in the fridge. Use 3 Tbsp. each day in your recipes and dressings (great in Oil & Vinegar French Dressing) and sauces. It stores in the fridge for 5-7 days.

Although this recipe is for plain, unflavored seed cheese, you can add any vegetable, onion, garlic, or seasoning to the soaked seeds. Put them in the blender with the seeds and the Rejuvelac and let the flavors mellow together while you are processing the cheese.

After you learn how to make Rejuvelac and seed cheese, you can create your own style and varieties. If you are having trouble adjusting the flavors to suit your taste, just keep working at it. The result will be worth the effort, especially in terms of taste and the quality of food value that these foods carry to your cells. Plus, these foods are rich in enzymes and living healthy bacteria that they supply to your intestinal tract...without the milk or lactose!

Balancing act

You may read some conflicting information about the live bacteria in seed cheese and Rejuvelac. I truly believe, through blood analysis, that fermented foods create alkalinity in the body. I experimented by staying off fermented foods for a few years, during which time I ate only 100% raw foods. After eight months, I noticed that my digestive tract began to slow down, and by the end of eighteen months—even with quarterly body cleansing, sufficient water, and eating water-rich living foods—my eliminative system was becoming more and more sluggish. I began to integrate Rejuvelac back into my diet. Within four days I was experiencing a substantial improvement in my system, not only my eliminative system, but also my energy, stamina and digestion. Within a week, I began to make seed cheese and started to eat 3 Tbsp. everyday with my salads. My strength, clarity and sustained energy returned. Work and exercise flowed smoothly again, whereas I had felt totally exhausted at the end of the day without it.

For six months, I ate these fermented foods as I had done before, but now I was reaping the complete-ness that I had been lacking despite the fact that I had been eating 100% living foods and drinking 4 oz. of fresh wheatgrass juice everyday. Without the fermented foods, I felt that something was lacking. Later that sum-mer, I took a microscopy certification class and, in my live blood cell analysis, I discovered there was no added bacteria, acid, or parasitical content in my blood; rather, I had only healthy round cells that were fully absorbing the nutrients and oxygen from the living foods that I was eating. The live fermented foods assisted in balancing and eliminating toxins from my blood, which manifested health and vibrancy in my skin, organs and body.

Remember, fermented foods aid in digestion. As a baby, the original flora in your intestines is usually supplied by the disulfide in your mother's milk. That flora would last a lifetime were it not for dietary abuse that depletes the friendly bacteria. Fermented foods help restore and strengthen those bacteria. Seed cheese and Rejuvelac are valuable sources of acidophilus, bifidis, living enzymes and electrolytes. Three table-spoons of seed cheese everyday is optimal for adults. Plain, unflavored seed cheese is so delicious when it is added to Oil & Vinegar French Dressing and eaten with your salad at lunchtime. You receive a sense of satisfaction and fullness that a raw food or vegetarian diet sometimes lacks.

If you are an athlete in training or just beginning a workout schedule, your body will be stressed. Use more seed cheese, which is a high source of protein and amino acid complexes. Your rejuvelac functions like a powered-up electrolyte drink, without the added salt and sugar. Use these valuable energy foods to sustain, build and repair your body as you get in or stay in shape. When you add seed cheese to raw crackers or breads, keep the dehydration temperature of 105° F so the living nutrition stays intact. Enjoy these new possibilities!

Pepper/Squash Seed Pizza
Mix:

>   2 cups seed cheese
>
>   4 cloves pressed garlic
>
>   1 bunch parsley, minced
>
>   1 bunch green onions, minced
>
>   3 stalks celery, minced
>
>   1 bunch basil and oregano, minced
>
>   2 Tbsp. raw honey
>
>   2 Tbsp. Nama Shoyu
>
>   2 Tbsp. healthy ketchup, (optional)
>
>   2 Tbsp. Italian seasoning herbs
>
>   Spike and "Real Salt" (to taste)

Serving options:

Spoon onto red pepper boats, or corner-cut zucchini, ¼" thick.

Top with fresh basil leaf or slice of tomato with Spike, or both!

Dehydrate at 105° F for 4-6 hours.

Serve moist. Dehydrate until crisp to save for backpacking.

These will give you a lot of added energy in the out-of-doors.

Quick Altitude Pizza (Shortcut Version)

Add to 2 cups of seed cheese:

    Onion powder and garlic powder

    Basil and oregano

    Spike, and salt and pepper (optional)

    Nama Shoyu or Kikkoman

    Vicki's Oil and Vinegar French Dressing (optional)

Spread on zucchini slices.

Dehydrate overnight.

These are quick and easy. Good recipe for bachelors and food on the go.

Easy Seed Cheese Dressing

In a small bowl mix:

    3 Tbsp. seed cheese

    Add "Easy Oil and Vinegar Dressing" until desired consistency.

Note: this dressing doesn't keep well because of the living seed cheese.

Mix up one serving at a time.

Serve immediately on your salad.

Easy Oil and Vinegar Dressing

    1 cup oil, (you can use some Rejuvelac here instead)

    ½ cup apple cider vinegar

    ¼ cup Nama Shoyu

    A 6-second squirt of ketchup

    A 2-second squirt of mustard

Shake 30 times.

Keeps in fridge indefinitely.

Seed Cheese Breads and Crackers

For a little more protein and a feeling of fullness, add seed cheese to your living crackers and manna breads. Here are a few of my favorites:

Spicy Seed Bread

Run through Champion Juicer with a blank:

    1 cup soaked almonds

    2 cups sprouted wheat

    1 cup soaked sunflower seeds

    1 cup soaked pumpkin seeds

Alternate with:

    8 carrots

    Green or red pepper

    6 cloves of garlic

    1 fresh ginger

Set dough aside.

Mince:

    1 red pepper

    5 stalks celery

    1 bunch green onions

    1 bunch fresh basil

    1 bunch fresh oregano

Mix together and add:

    1 cup seed cheese

½ cup each soaked sunflower and flax seeds

1 Tbsp. caraway seeds

½ cup Nama Shoyu or Kikkoman Soy sauce

Spike to taste

Form into patties.

Dehydrate at 105° F for 3-4 hours.

Then turn for another 2-3 hours.

Italian Protein Crackers (very high in assimilable proteins)

2 cups rye sprouts

½ cup garbanzo bean sprouts

½ cup pea sprouts

½ cup sunflower sprouts

½ cup sprouted sesame seeds

½ cup seed cheese

2 stalks celery

½ small onion

1 red pepper

4 Tbsp. Nama Shoyu or Kikkoman

3 sprigs each fresh basil, oregano, and parsley

3-4 Tbsp. Italian seasoning

2 tsp. cumin

Spike to taste

Blend until smooth, then add 3 chopped tomatoes.

Pulse 3 times so tomatoes are chunky.

Pour onto solid dehydrator sheets.

Dehydrate at 105° F overnight or until crisp.

COMMITTED
CREATIVITY
IS THE MOTHER OF
GOURMET FOODS.

Chapter 10

Sprouted Nut Butters and Milks

Healthy "Mock" Peanut Butter

Most of us grew up with the belief that peanut butter was good for us. Now we are learning how toxic commercial peanuts are. Many people have allergic reactions to peanuts and peanut products. Additionally, most of the nut butters in health food stores, even the ones you grind yourself, are so roasted there isn't any nutrition left. What are we to do? We have been taught that peanut butter is a healthy staple. We make peanut butter and jelly (or honey) sandwiches, which are a terribly improper food combination—eating a protein (like peanut butter) and a starch (like bread) creates a fast sugar in the pancreas, which causes insulin to jump dangerously high; the combination can also create a bowel blockage over time.

There is a healthier choice.

Again, sprouted seeds and nuts come to the rescue. Really, any combination of your favorites can be used. Mock Peanut Butter is a perfect addition to your children's diet. The elderly can benefit as well, especially those who have trouble chewing. Because the seeds are sprouted and the proteins are now in plant form, you can easily spread this "butter" on a piece of your own sprouted Manna Bread, and it won't qualify as an improper food combination of grains and starches—the butter is a plant protein and the grain is a plant starch. Note: If you begin to gain weight with the Manna Bread and Mock Peanut Butter, you may have to cut back and indulge only a few times each week...*after* eating a large greens salad!

Every so often I work with someone who can't keep weight on. In this case, you can try 3-4 Tbsp. of the seed cheese at each meal. Add 3-4 Tbsp. of Mock

Peanut Butter with Manna Bread after eating your huge *greens* salad with some thick living dressings on it. This provides a healthy amount of fats and proteins that the body *can* digest and assimilate, while sustaining or building weight.

If you are recovering from starvation or a degenerative illness that has brought you down and you are trying to rebuild your body, eat 3-4 Tbsp. of this soaked nut combination several times a day. It is very high in whole food minerals, vitamins, proteins and fats. This and seed cheese are great ways to gain some healthy weight.

Mock Peanut Butter (without the peanuts!)
½ cup sesame seeds, soaked overnight
¾ cup sunflower seeds, soaked
½ cup pumpkin seeds, soaked
½ cup flax seeds, soaked
1 cup whole wheat, sprouted
1 cup almonds, soaked 48 hours
½ cup quinoa, sprouted
½ cup whole rye, sprouted
1 cup shelled Brazil Nuts, soaked 48 hours
Raw honey or 4-8 pitted and soaked dates
1-2 Tbsp. pure vanilla (to taste)
1-2 tsp. almond extract
Cinnamon and nutmeg (optional)

Directions:

Sprout wheat, rye and millet 2-3 days before, until the tails are about ½ as large as the grain.

Soak the almonds and Brazil Nuts 2 days before.

Soak all other small seeds overnight.

Blend until smooth. (For smoothness, I like using my Vita Mix for this recipe.)

Store in the refrigerator. Chop up and add soaked almonds and walnuts for "chunky" style.

Because this is a living food, use it up in two weeks.

A quick, energy snack. Tastes great on all raw crackers and breads, rice cakes, rice crackers.

Put on top of apple slices or celery boats.

Use in any recipe calling for peanut butter.

Raw Almond Butter

   2 cups soaked almonds (48 hours)

Add:

   Honey, soaked dates or maple syrup (to taste)

   1-2 tsp. each real vanilla and almond extracts

   Enough liquid or Rejuvelac to make a butter

Blend in Vita Mix until creamy and smooth.

Spread on a solid dehydrator sheet and dehydrate at 105° F for 2 hours.

Turn with a spatula, and dehydrate for 2 hours more using the spatula to stir it as it thickens.

Use as nut butter on veggies, crackers, and Manna Bread, or use as almond butter in "Gorf" recipes for hiking and backpacking.

"Gorf" Mix (Trail Mix or Energy Bar)

1-2 cups fresh raw almond butter (Health Food Store nut butters are cooked)

½ cup honey, maple syrup, blended soaked dates, etc.

¼ - ½ cup date sugar

½ cup unsweetened coconut

¼ cup raw peanuts, pine nuts, sunflower seeds, etc., soaked overnight

½ cup soaked almonds or larger nuts, chopped

½ cup raisins, dried cranberries, date pieces, etc.

¼ cup raw carob powder (optional)

½ cup vegan carob chips (optional)

Press into bars or balls and eat immediately!

Or dehydrate at 105° F and use as a power bar.

Sprouted "Milks"

As a society, we truly overuse milk. There are myriad ailments that easily could be eliminated by reducing or cutting out lactose-rich milk. Sprouted milks can easily substitute for conventional milk in the daily diet.

If you are looking for extra calcium in your diet, soaked sesame seeds are the richest source of calcium.

Milks make from soaked sesame seeds and sprouted soy beans can easily fulfill your calcium needs. Also, almonds, Brazil Nuts and sunflower seeds are rich sources of protein and calcium as well.

True soymilk is made with soaked and lightly sprouted soybeans. The sweeteners are your preference. Raw honey works for some people; pure *Grade B* maple syrup works for others; and still other people prefer soaking and pitting fresh dates then blending them up to sweeten their sprouted milks. Use pure vanilla and pure almond extracts to make the flavor rich tasting.

These milks are wonderful on cereals and also in drinks. Sprouted cereal with almond milk on top is like eating a dessert for breakfast, and it will carry you throughout the morning with plenty of energy; with none of that sluggishness that you feel after eating sugary cereals.

Soaking almonds, nuts and seeds brings out the proteins and diminishes the fat. Once you have tasted 48-hour soaked almonds, you probably won't go back to plain almonds (which are very acidic before they are soaked).

Think of all of the extra nutrition you are giving your family instead of all of the mucus-forming fat! Have fun with these recipes!

Almond Milk
Fill the blender blades with soaked almonds

Add:

> 2 cups water (the more water the thinner the milk)
>
> 1-2 tsp. real vanilla
>
> ½ tsp. pure almond flavor
>
> 2 tsp. raw honey or 3-5 soaked dates
>
> 2 shakes of cinnamon (optional)
>
> Ice cubes

Blend

You can substitute any nut or seed for the almonds.

Holiday Nutmeg Nog—Raw

> 2 cups sprouted almonds (soaked 48 hours)
>
> 2 cups water (less, if you want it thicker)
>
> Honey or soaked dates (to taste)
>
> 2 tsp. real vanilla
>
> 1 tsp. pure almond oil
>
> 1 tsp. fresh nutmeg (or more to taste)
>
> Pinch or two of cinnamon
>
> Handful of ice

Blend in the blender.

Serve while frothy. Sprinkle fresh Nutmeg on top.

Note: If you don't like the soaked almond skins, pinch them off before blending.

Raspberry Almond Milk Shake

In a blender:

> 2 cups soaked almonds
>
> Fill blender ½ full with water

½ cup raw honey or soaked dates (to taste)

2 tsp. vanilla

1 tsp. almond flavoring

Blend until smooth then add:

2 bananas

1 cup fresh or frozen raspberries

Enough ice to desired thickness

Enjoy!

Mock Chocolate Milk

Blend:

2 cups fresh almond milk (see recipe)

2-3 tsp. raw carob powder

1 Tbsp. honey or 4-5 soaked-pitted dates (to taste)

1-2 tsp. real vanilla

1 tsp. pure almond oil

Pinch of nutmeg

Adjust any ingredient for your own unique taste.

HEALING
TRULY TAKES PLACE
WHEN WE HAVE
HANDS-ON
COMMITMENT
TO OUR OWN HEALTH.

Chapter II

Growing Grains and Greens

When the sprouts begin to reach the stage that they turn green and grow a tiny stem, they are no longer used for eating but they need to grow. In the winter, you can prolong the growing season by sprouting and growing wheatgrass and greens right in your own kitchen. Few things taste as good as un-refrigerated, fresh greens harvested at just the perfect stage. Throughout the summer, you still may be sprouting a little, but most of the summertime greens and wheatgrass will be grown in your outside garden. Let's first explore how to grow them in the kitchen.

You will need:

> 10 growing trays
>
> Organic soil to fill up to ¾ inch from the bottom of the tray
>
> 2-3 cups sprouted wheat

Growing Sprouted Wheat (Grown Inside)

1. Before beginning, moisten the soil in a bucket. You can use organic soil purchased at a nursery or topsoil from your outside garden. (Topsoil is the first foot of soil. Compost is the most desirable soil.)

2. Spread the soil evenly in the growing tray. You only need ½ - ¾" of soil.

3. Sprinkle the moist soil with kelp granules, or you can dissolve kelp granules or powder in water. To prevent mold, water the soil once or twice in seven days with this mixture.

4. Thickly and evenly, spread the sprouts over the soil. The grains will touch each other. If the sprouts seem too thick, the consistency is probably just right.

5. Water the sprouts lightly from a fine spray watering can.

6. Cover the sprouted wheat with another empty tray and let it sit on the counter.

7. For the first two days, remove the empty tray to water, and spray light mist on the sprouts daily— until the empty tray on the top rises an inch or two with the baby grass stem growing underneath.

8. Take off the tray so the little stems can now get some light. Water well once a day until the wheatgrass is about seven inches long.

9. Now it's time to harvest the grass. Take a handful of the growing wheatgrass; use scissors or a knife to cut as close to the dirt as possible without pulling up the roots.

10. Put the grass into your wheatgrass juicer press and drink immediately.

Use only one cutting then compost or throw away the mat. When you are growing in ½" of soil, there will not be enough nutrition for a second cutting.

If you are drinking 4 oz. everyday, you will probably use a whole flat of wheatgrass each day. If your wheatgrass is thick, you might get more juice from the wheatgrass flats. Run the wheatgrass pulp through the juicer 5-6 times to extract as much of the juice as possible. Try practicing growing the flats before you become too dependent on the daily amounts you will consume. Purchase some flats at the health food store to help you through your learning curve.

You can make a wheatgrass growing shelf out of teakwood or PVC pipe. Make 6-7 shelves that the trays can sit on. In this way, you can bring up each tray everyday until you are rotating seven trays. When you start your first tray, place it on the bottom shelf. The next day, bring it up a shelf and start a new tray, which goes on the bottom shelf. Continue moving up each tray until you reach seven. When all of them are growing, you now can start harvesting the oldest one. For every tray you harvest, start a new one. Soon, kitchen gardening will become a part of your daily routine. Since you will be starting a tray everyday, you need to make sure you are also soaking and sprouting your wheat sprouts everyday. Your stackable sprouting trays will keep your countertop neat and organized.

Sprouted Wheat (Grown Outside)

Sprout the 2 cups of wheat, just like you would in the kitchen.

Prepare a strip of earth about 2 feet wide by 8 feet long. Make sure that the soil is worked and composted with lots of good nutrients.

Divide the strip into 7 sections. Arrange the sprouts, very thickly, on a 2-foot x 1-foot section; water, and cover with an empty sprouting tray.

Plant the next section the next day. Continue planting another section everyday until all 7 sections are planted.

Take the empty trays off of the baby wheat when it is about 1 inch tall.

By the time the last tray area is planted, the first tray area will be ready to harvest.

Cut the wheatgrass with a knife when it is about 7 inches tall. Cut the grass as close to the soil as possible without damaging the root system. Allow the wheatgrass to re-grow for more cuttings throughout the summer and fall.

With this method, you will use a section each day, and by the time you get to the last section, the first section is ready to be cut again. This insures that you will have plenty of wheatgrass on hand as you need it. If you have any left over, cut it when it reaches about 7 inches then store in the fridge in an airtight bag.

Feed your soil with an organic mineral or bacteria to keep the nutrition content in your wheatgrass high. Water once in awhile with kelp powder dissolved in water.

If your wheatgrass starts to burn from intense sun exposure, hang garden netting over the wheatgrass to protect it.

Growing Buckwheat, Sunflower, Pea Greens & Herbs (grown inside)

These greens can be substituted for lettuces and greens. These are excellent sources of protein, calcium, and chlorophyll. In an emergency, when other greens might not be available, use these greens for your daily salads. They taste great; they are fresh and crunchy; and they provide much nutrition and minerals to your body everyday. They are easy to grow, so you can do it yourself. Here are types of greens that you can grow:

- Sunflower greens. Use un-hulled sunflower seeds, preferably solid black. These provide a complete protein.
- Buckwheat greens. Use un-hulled seeds. These are full of lecithin, which is a powerful brain food.
- Pea greens. Use un-cooked, raw, whole peas. These are full of minerals.

Follow the same pattern as you would to grow wheatgrass indoors. Use the same system with the empty tray on the top. You will probably use about half the tray of each week's growth, so double up on the types of seeds that you grow in each tray. Basil, oregano, parsley, cilantro, rosemary, etc. can be grown in a small pot throughout the winter. Water lightly once a day, and harvest the herbs continually so you can use them in your salads. In early summer, transplant these herbs to your garden, preferably in a moist, partially shady spot. In the late fall before the first frost, cut them down to dirt level then take the remaining herb plant—roots and all—to get starts for your winter kitchen garden. Now the cycle continues.

~Recipes~

Sunflower, Lentil and Basil Salad

Grate:

Jicama, zucchini, yellow squash and carrots

Add:

1 small red onion, sliced

1 tomato, diced

1 avocado, cubed

1 cup soaked sunflower seeds

1 cup each buckwheat, peas and sunflower greens, chopped

1 cup of barely sprouted red lentil sprouts

1 bunch fresh basil leaves, chopped

Top with Vicki's "Oil and Vinegar French" or "Creamy French Dressing."

Sunflower Salad

Grate:

1 jicama

1 zucchini

2 raw yams, peeled

Press:

    2 cloves of garlic

    ½ inch fresh ginger, peeled

Add:

    3 Roma tomatoes, chopped

    4 cups sunflower greens, chopped (or any greens)

    1 cup sunflower seeds, soaked overnight

    1-2 cups fresh basil, chopped

    1 cup green onion, chopped

    2 avocados, firm to the touch, cubed

Add:

    Spring Mix

    Fresh spinach

    Any raw deep leafy greens

Toss all ingredients together carefully. Marinate in the "Oil and Vinegar French Dressing" or your favorite balsamic vinaigrette dressing. Enjoy!

Growing Lettuces and Spinach

    Just like the other greens, herbs, and wheatgrass, lettuces can also be grown in trays in your kitchen. These seeds need to be soaked overnight, and when you spread them on the trays, spread a small layer of soil over the top of the soaked seeds. The baby lettuces are especially sweet. You can buy varieties of Spring Mix or experiment with the different flavors to make your favorite mix. The kitchen looks so pretty when all of the greens are maturing!

Outside growing of lettuces, spinach, kale, Swiss chard, collards, etc., requires very little maintenance. Plant the seeds directly in the soil early in the spring. The deep leafy greens are very hearty and can withstand cold temperatures. Plan ahead for the summer when the sun may burn the leaf of the greens by choosing a spot that can be covered, if needed, with garden netting.

Whether or not you grow indoors or outdoors, creating your own food *changes* how you will look at food. There is a wonderful difference in the taste of something you have grown with your own hands. You develop a respect and a curiosity for the earth, and the miracle of new growth signals to your body that what you are going to feed it—will heal it.

Growing greens

Experiment with these important foods—*Greens.* I refer to all salads as "greens salads" because I want you understand that every good salad is served on a bed of greens. Greens are typically defined as the deep leafy greens: *Kale,* either curly or non-curly Lucinato; *Swiss Chard,* all colors of stems; *Beet tops,* cut off of fresh beets; *Collard greens,* with their huge leaves; *Mustard greens,* with the spicy-hot flavor; and *Dandelion greens* (see Chapter 13).

Whether you are a veteran *raw food* person or a novice who is just getting started on a healthy diet, it is important that you eat a large "greens salad" before you eat anything else for lunch and dinner. If the flavors are not yet desirable, use the Lemon Tahini Dressing mixed with a sweet dressing like Poppyseed Dressing, or Creamy Sprouted French Dressing, any of which you can pour abundantly over your salads to create a taste that you'll love. Dressings help to get the good greens down in the beginning. There is no prize for eating salads without dressing. Feel free to indulge.

And then there are oils. Some people don't want to use oils with raw foods, but oils are an essential for the diet. Cold pressed oils are recommended. Take a look at the blended dressings below—the ratio of oils to amounts of vegetables is small. So allow yourself permission to enjoy your salads. Learn to love these foods that will build your body.

Greens are not created equal. There are many types. Leafy, deep leafy greens, or "greens" as I call them, have more protein and calcium than lighter colored "greens." Have you noticed when you eat a greens salad full of the deep leafy greens, you feel more satisfied? That's because there was more food value in the greens. As with any food transition, if you are feeling hungry, try adding to your salads some deep leafy greens and one of these thick blended dressings. You will experience more satisfaction. If the taste is too bitter or too *green,* try adding a *small* amount of finely chopped deep greens. The non-curly Lucinato kale that is available in health food stores is a good transition green because it is deep, leafy and sweeter than the other greens.

As I have said before, eat a big greens salad at the beginning of your lunch and dinner. This will make the difference between your just feeling good and for your *permanent* health. *First-eaten* salads will help to rebuild your body's cellular structure, and repair and support your immune system for future disease prevention.

Have fun with your salads! In the beginning, you may not feel excited about eating so much salad in your daily diet. So ease into the practice. Start with one salad a day then progress soon to two salads, which is a great accomplishment. The time may come when you become bored with your salads. You'll need to work on being more creative. New dressings become important. Combinations of greens and dressings provide almost endless tastes. Watch my website and my publications for more and more "cook" books that will contain lots of dressings and salad ideas. After a cleanse (with the 3 days of juice meals), your taste buds are also cleansed. You discover yourself craving salads and raw dressings. Amazing what you crave when there isn't rotten material in your body!

Remember, at whatever stage you are at, "food is fuel." One of the best ways to permanent, optimal health is the consistent daily consumption of living foods. As you perfect your flavor-mixing skills, you *will* discover the wonderful and delicious world of living foods. Keep experimenting and creating new flavor sensations for your salads, and enjoy!

Yummy Salad Meal Ideas

Wash and cut:

> Green leaf and Red leaf lettuce
>
> Romaine lettuce
>
> Kale, curly and non-curly Lucinato
>
> Swiss chard, all colors
>
> Collard greens, uncooked

Chop:

> Buckwheat, sunflower, pea greens, Baby Spring Mix, Baby Spinach, etc.

Grate:

> Carrots
>
> Beets
>
> Zucchini
>
> Squash, etc.

Slice:

> Cucumbers
>
> Green Pepper
>
> Tomatoes
>
> Mushrooms, etc.

Chop:

> Broccoli
>
> Jicima
>
> Cauliflower

Avocado

Any raw veggie you like

Toss all together and serve with any of "Vicki's Delicious Dressings".

When you begin making and enjoying these delicious salads and dressings, you truly will desire to "wash, cut, chop, grate, slice and chop" again and again!

Deep Green Mexi Salad

Chop:

Fresh Spring Mix and spinach

Mince:

Swiss chard

Fresh kale and fresh basil

Add:

Red onion slices

Red pepper strips

Grated carrots

Toss together and serve with Mexican Vinaigrette.

Mexican Vinaigrette

1 cup olive oil

½ cup fresh lemon juice

½ cup apple cider vinegar

1" ginger, pressed

4 cloves minced garlic

3 Tbsp. Nama Shoyu, or Kikkoman Soy sauce

1 sprig chopped fresh basil

1 sprig chopped fresh cilantro

½ tsp. oregano

¼ red pepper, chopped

½ tsp. cumin

½ raw jalapeno, minced (optional)

Shake and serve. You can blend this too.

Toss for the Mexi Salad, or use as a general salad dressing.

Keeps in the fridge for about 7-10 days.

Protein Lettuce Salad

Spring Mix and fresh baby spinach

Shredded red and green cabbage

Chopped broccoli

Soaked pine nuts

Red onion

Cucumbers

Tomatoes

Mix and serve with sprouted Creamy Sprouted French Dressing.

Sprout Salad with Mint

Red lentil sprouts, soaked overnight

Green lentil sprouts, sprouted 3-4 days

Brown sesame seed sprouts, soaked overnight

Garbanzo sprouts, sprouted 1-2 days

Pea sprouts, sprouted 2-3 days

3 handfuls spring lettuce mix

2 chopped tomatoes

1 bunch peppermint, chopped

Toss with any of Vicki's homemade dressings.

Sesame Ginger Greens

Chop:

Fresh Spring Mix and baby spinach

Minced non-curly Lucinato kale and Swiss chard

Fresh pea pods

1 red pepper cut in strips

Sliced red onion

1 cup mung bean sprouts

1 cup soaked sesame seeds

Toss and serve with Sesame Ginger Dressing.

Sesame Ginger Dressing

2 Tbsp. cold pressed sesame oil

2 Tbsp. brown rice vinegar

3 Tbsp. Rejuvelac or water

2 Tbsp. Nama Shoyu or Kikkoman

1 clove garlic, pressed

½" fresh ginger, pressed

2 Tbsp. fresh lemon juice

3 Tbsp. finely minced sweet onion

Pinch of "Real Salt" (optional)

Mix with a wire whisk or blend.

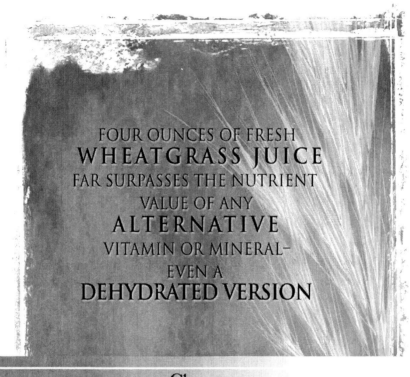

FOUR OUNCES OF FRESH
WHEATGRASS JUICE
FAR SURPASSES THE NUTRIENT
VALUE OF ANY
ALTERNATIVE
VITAMIN OR MINERAL–
EVEN A
DEHYDRATED VERSION

Chapter 12

The Wonderful World
of Wheatgrass

Wheatgrass Juice

Dr. Ann Wigmore first introduced wheatgrass to the world forty years ago. She was looking for a food substance that would nourish the body at the cellular level. She first began by chewing wheatgrass to extract the juice, and later she used a juice press to extract more of this nourishing substance. She discovered that the properties of wheatgrass juice cleansed the body of toxins and nourished the system. She knew that any natural substance first cleanses the body before rebuilding it; the body will not build upon filth. Achieving true health is first to cleanse out the filth, then release foreign substances, and *as a final point,* to rebuild the system by daily supporting the body's cells with cellular foods. This is especially important information for those who suffer or have suffered addictions, chronic pain or an "incurable" illness. Dr. Wigmore discovered that wheatgrass juice is an excellent stimulus to initiate and support detoxification.

What is Wheatgrass juice and what are its benefits?

Wheatgrass is the young wheat plant that grows from a wheat sprout. The grass is harvested prior to the jointing stage, in which the grass leaf begins to form a stem. At this stage the wheatgrass is considered a vegetable rather than a grain; it is at the peak of the plant's vegetative development. Juicing the wheatgrass unlocks important nutrients, concentrating them into a form that the body can easily absorb. Interestingly, many people, who are wheat or gluten-sensitive—after they have been consistently cleansing their bodies every three months—may discover that neither wheatgrass juice nor wheat sprouts bother them.

Wheatgrass juice contains over ninety alkalizing minerals that are needed to maintain good metabolism. These minerals include calcium, magnesium, and potassium. Additionally, wheatgrass juice contains an adequate amount of iron, which is an organic mineral essential for transporting oxygen to the lungs. The iron in wheatgrass juice does not constipate the intestines. Wheatgrass juice also contains organic sodium, imperative to improving digestion and the regulation of body fluids. Conversely, commercialized foods contain low to no organic minerals. Worse, our soils have been depleted of these minerals and nutrients over the past fifty years. Little wonder that people who consume commercially sold vegetables find that these foods lack the organic minerals that are necessary for basic physiological function. Depletion of essential minerals can render the body incapable of burning fats and metabolizing normally. For instance, depleted levels of chromium in the soil upset the body's ability to metabolize fats, which can contribute to weight gain and even obesity. Wheatgrass juice and organic foods can replenish chromium and reestablish true metabolic function.

With wheatgrass's powerhouse combination of nutrients, minerals, and other healthy agents, wheatgrass is said to build the body's strength so it can better combat, cleanse, repair and heal the body's systems and counteract many symptoms of weakness or illness. You may discover that the wheatgrass juice creates within you an *environment* of healing (see disclaimer on Copyright page). Here are some health benefits that I have personally experienced over the last fourteen years by drinking 4 oz. of fresh wheatgrass each day.

Wheatgrass juice can supply organic sodium, which is necessary to maintain the hydrochloric acid balance in the stomach for digestion. Digestive problems, heartburn, and acid stomach can be negative results of lack of the hydrochloric acid. Drinking water, soda pop and milk at dinnertime can lead to dilution of hydrochloric acid, which lack can affect digestion and waste elimination. Drinking your water and juice one hour before and after meals diminishes the amount of hydrochloric acid dilution. And drinking one cup of freshly juiced organic celery everyday over a month could replace some of the lost organic sodium. Drinking four ounces of fresh wheatgrass juice could also assist in reestablishing the body's acid/alkaline balance, which creates an environment for the body to reset and emit the nutrients, agents and acids that are necessary for healthy physical functions.

Wheatgrass juice doubles as an internal deodorant. Drinking the juice exposes fresh chlorophyll to negative bacteria starting from the tongue all the way through the digestive system. Bad breath could be eliminated over time, through drinking four ounces of wheatgrass juice daily. The chlorophyll in wheatgrass juice opens the possibilities for the body to cleanse and rebuild the bloodstream, refine the tissues, purify the liver to wash drug deposits from the body, and neutralize toxins throughout the body. Because chlorophyll is anti-bacterial, it can be used in and outside the body.

Wheatgrass juice can assist the body in reversing and correcting blood sugar problems by diminishing cravings for fast sugars, dissolving sugar-rich mucous deposits, and creating an environment for the pancreas to heal. When you drink wheatgrass juice, you usually don't crave sugars. When you are eating a lot of sugars, you usually don't want to drink your wheatgrass juice!

Wheatgrass juice can assist the body to refine the elasticin on the inside and outside of your skin, creating strong organ systems, healthy glowing skin, and decreasing cellulite.

Swishing wheatgrass juice between your teeth could possibly aid in preventing tooth decay and strengthening gums and tooth enamel. And wheatgrass juice works on eliminating bad breath!

Strained wheatgrass juice can be used in an eye-cup to clean the eye and possibly dissolve eye mucus.

Wheatgrass juice can be snorted up one nostril at a time to clean out the sinuses and to release infection trapped in the sinus cavities.

Wheatgrass juice has been said to release heavy metals from the body, cleanse pollutants from the body, and release radiation.

In this day and age, wheatgrass juice seems to be the perfect combatant against environmental and physiological attack, the best protective whole food, and the perfect food for today's world. Wheatgrass juice — "wheat for man" is more than a truism.

Wheatgrass juice and chlorophyll

Wheatgrass juice is rich in chlorophyll, which acts as a magnet that draws toxins out from the body. Chlorophyll can cleanse the tissues and sooth and heal them at the same time. The photosynthesis process, whose source is the sun, creates chlorophyll, which when fired by organic minerals, supercharges wheatgrass juice into light and oxygen. Clearly, wheatgrass juice is liquid oxygen and liquid light.

Dr. Klinic Bircher-Benner says, "Absorption and organization of sunlight, the very essence of life, is almost exclusively derived from plants. Plants are therefore a biological accumulation of light. Since light is the driving force of every cell in your bodies, that is why we need plants."

The wheatgrass juice molecule is similar to human blood molecules. The primary exceptions are the core of blood is iron and the core of wheatgrass juice is magnesium. The body needs magnesium to absorb amino acids, which are the building blocks of life. The magnesium in wheatgrass juice is built into the blood and assists the body to absorb all of the amino acids (proteins) to then carry those nutrients and precious oxygen to the cells. Wheatgrass juice is a pure living source of fresh chlorophyll.

Wheatgrass juice and enzymes

Wheatgrass juice is filled with enzymes, which are the life force that we need to carry out many important chemical and biological functions in the body. Enzymes are destroyed by excessive heat that is commonly used to process many of today's foods. Additionally, wheatgrass juice contains:

- *Protease,* which assists in digesting protein
- *Cytochrome Oxidase,* which is an anti-oxidant used for cell restoration
- *Amylase,* which facilitates starch digestion
- *Lipase,* which is a fat-splitting enzyme
- *Transhydrogenase,* which keeps the muscle tissue of the heart toned
- *Superoxide Dismutase,* which is found in all body cells and which slows cellular aging.

Our bodies benefit greatly if at least 50% of our diet is enzyme-rich food. Wheatgrass juice more than qualifies to be an active part of your daily eating habits.

Wheatgrass juice every day

Every electrolyte, enzyme and amino acid that the body needs is found in four ounces of fresh wheatgrass juice. This makes wheatgrass juice a complete protein. Along with essential amino acids, it contains:

- *Alanine,* which builds the blood
- *Aspartic Acid,* which converts food to energy
- *Glutamic Acid,* which improves mental balance and function
- *Serine,* which stimulates brain and nerve function.

Just four ounces of fresh wheatgrass juice per day is a reliable and necessary source for Vegans, Vegetarians, and Raw Food People, to consistently obtain their daily protein consumption.

Typically, we recommend beginning the use of wheatgrass juice after finishing a two-week cleanse that involves 3-4 colonics. This process allows the toxins, which wheatgrass juice stimulates the body to release, to be easily removed from the body and to greatly increase the possibility of reducing any uncomfortable cleansing reactions.

How do I start drinking wheatgrass juice?

Begin by drinking just one ounce of wheatgrass juice each day.

Do this for one week. Then do:

2 oz/day for the 2nd week

3 oz/day for the 3rd week, and

4 oz/day thereafter.

It is not necessary to drink more than 4 oz/each day.

It is preferable to drink wheatgrass juice an hour before you eat. But if you can't or if you feel nauseated, you can follow drinking the juice with a slice of orange or a piece of a banana, then follow that with a fresh blender drink or a salad. Remember, the characteristic of wheatgrass juice is to dissolve mucus in thirty seconds then release that toxic mucus out of the body in the quickest way possible. If you are feeling sick or nauseated, you need to understand that the wheatgrass juice is *not* what is making you sick; the mucus is making you sick; the wheatgrass juice is doing its job. It is dissolving mucous food, such as sugars, deep fried foods, chocolate, breads, potatoes, etc., and removing that mucus from the body.

If you are drinking wheatgrass juice, you are probably not craving sweets and junky foods. If you are not drinking wheatgrass juice, you are most likely eating *only* sweets and junky foods. Wheatgrass juice curbs sugary cravings if you drink it on a consistent, day-to-day basis.

How do I press the wheatgrass juice?

You have to use an agar-type press to press your wheatgrass juice. Wheatgrass is too fibrous to use in a centrifugal force juicer, and it can be hard on expensive all-inclusive juicers. The best juicer to use to get the most juice from a flat of wheatgrass is a hand or manual juicer. In this type of juicer, you can put back the juiced pulp about six times. (For more information, see my website: www.VickiTalmage.com.)

How do I get wheatgrass?

You can buy wheatgrass in flats at a health food store. One flat usually yields about seven ounces of juice, or one ounce of wheatgrass juice for everyday of the week. You can buy wheatgrass already cut in bags, or the cheapest way to buy wheatgrass is grow it in your own home or garden (growing kits are available online). You can grow a flat of wheatgrass for about 20 cents per flat. If you store wheat, now is the time to get it out and use it.

What do I do if, after a while, I can't drink wheatgrass juice?

Sometimes the body is adverse to what is best for it. In those times, I have found that if I would take a deep breath and drink my 4 ounces at once then, once I swallowed it and before I took a breath, I would put a wedge of orange or a bite of banana in my mouth, the fruit taste would stimulate my sense of smell and cancel out the taste of the wheatgrass juice. Sometimes I had to eat a salad after drinking the juice.

Note: Don't mix the wheatgrass juice with other juices. Drink it alone, and drink it first before eating or drinking anything else. It is absorbed quickly in the mouth and esophagus. When you follow it with something such as fruit, you can rest assured that the wheatgrass has already been absorbed.

How long should I drink wheatgrass juice?
A lifetime.

GREENS
ARE THE
STAFF OF LIFE,
AND THE
HEALTHY
FOUNDATION
OF EVERY MEAL.

Chapter 13

Greens and Dressings—A Must!

Greens

The most important part of every meal is what you put into your mouth first. The brain defines everything you eat as soon as you begin to chew it. Make sure that your enzyme-rich foods are eaten first. The enzymes in these foods assist the body in breaking down the aggregations in the bowels. Make sure that 50% of your meal is raw, deep leafy greens.

Greens are full of calcium and protein. In fact, the deeper the green, the higher the content. All minerals are easily accessible to the body through the photosynthesis process. Two big salads with beds of deep leafy greens and loaded with any raw vegetable is a must for the *serious* advocate of permanent health. Greens are 75% protein; there is no other protein that can boast of such a high percentage of usable nutrition. Greens are the basis of cellular renewal.

In the beginning, you may not be accustomed to the flavor of greens. Use dressings to add flavor. There are many dressings that are thick and flavorful. You can use these plentifully to top your salads as you are adjusting to the flavors of the greens. Don't be afraid to mix and match the dressings to fit your taste and your satisfaction level. Eventually, you will be creating delicious salad meals, and you will become like countless others who would rather dine in because salads and dressings taste so much better at home!

As mentioned in this book, there are many types of greens around the world; each one has its own unique flavor. As you travel, go to the markets and try the different kinds of greens.

There are the lighter greens, such as romaine leaf lettuce, green leaf lettuce, red leaf lettuces, and bib lettuce.

There are the medium greens, such as spinach leaves and Spring Mix.

There are the deep leafy greens, such as kale (curly and non-curly Lucinato), Swiss Chards, mustard greens, collard greens, beet tops, and dandelion greens.

Preparing greens

Soak the greens in a sink of pure water to get out any sand. Rinse in a strainer then place them on a clean, dry towel, and gently roll them up in the towel to dry out the last of any moisture. Water breaks down the leaves; the more moisture that you can remove from the leaves the longer you can store them in the fridge.

Start by cutting up a bunch of each of the deep leafy greens and adding a head of the medium and light greens with them. Cut up the deep leafy greens tiny at first to give your mouth time to adjust to the new texture. Grate up red and green cabbage and carrots, too. The greens will be the consistent base for all of your salads.

You may want to cut up a large bowl of these basic greens and store them covered in the fridge all week. In this way, when you come home hungry, you can scoop some greens on a plate then add a chopped tomato and an avocado, pour on some dressing...and presto! You have a readymade meal in about three minutes. Food doesn't get any faster and healthier then this!

Deep leafy greens are perfect for traveling or living out of a cooler. If you can remove all the moisture from the leaves then store them uncut in airtight plastic bags, you can cut them up as you need them for each meal on your trip. The food stays fresher this way. Raw living foods will never hold you back from living fully.

Over time, you may discover that making your meals on demand becomes fast, and you will enjoy the fresh taste. You will also notice your food bill going down as you assimilate and integrate these high quality foods into your daily diet. You will discover your preference of which greens that you like, that you naturally want to rotate. You will never get bored of eating greens if you become a connoisseur of mixing dressings and flavors, combined with the myriad textures that the greens offer.

Here are some ideas:

Pomegranate Green Salad
Combine the following together:
   Spring Mix and baby spinach
   Kale and Swiss Chard
   1 bunch fresh basil
   Napa cabbage, chopped
   Raw butternut squash, grated
   1 cup pomegranate seeds
Toss together and Serve with Cranberry Vinaigrette

Bed of Greens

Chop:

> Romaine lettuce
>
> Kale
>
> Spinach
>
> Spring Mix
>
> Collard greens
>
> Napa cabbage
>
> Red cabbage

Keeps in fridge in an airtight container for over a week.

Dressings

Dressings can make or break a salad. Some people can eat salads without any dressing, or with a lemon, olive oil or balsamic vinegar. But these people are in the minority. Most people don't eat salads because they are healthy; most people eat salads because they are delicious. And dressings make healthy salads taste great!

Don't count the calories of dressings. If the dressings can introduce you to eating lots of greens, your body will soon begin to crave them and, over time, adjust to the amounts and types of dressings. If you want to stay away from dressings made of oils, you can substitute Rejuvelac for oil and use some blended, soaked seeds to provide a smoother, creamier consistency. Adjust the flavors to match your taste, and keep creating new flavors!

Classic Lemon Tahini Dressing

In a blender, fill the blender blades with brown sesame seeds. (Optional: You can soak them overnight then dehydrate them.)

Blend to cornmeal consistency.

Leave blender on and add:

> 1 cup cold-pressed oil
>
> Add juice of 1 lemon
>
> 1/8 – ¼ cup Nama Shoyu or Kikkoman Soy sauce
>
> 3-4 stalks celery, chopped
>
> ¼ small onion
>
> ½ red pepper
>
> A few dashes black pepper

Blend well until smooth.

Lasts 4-5 days in the fridge.

This dressing is the favorite among my friends and colleagues. It is great when it is made as thick as a raw veggie dip, especially when you eat it with strips of raw jicama and raw yam slices. Serve it as a spread on Manna Bread and raw crackers, as a dip, or as a salad dressing mixed with the Easy Oil and Vinegar French, Poppy Seed, or the Creamy Sprouted French dressings. This dressing is versatile and satisfying. Enjoy!

Poppy Seed Dressing

Best if made in the same blender after the Lemon Tahini (don't rinse it out!)

> 1 cup cold-pressed oil

¼-½ cup raw apple cider vinegar

¼ cup honey

¼ small onion

2-3 stalks celery, chopped

1-2 tsp. Favorite Mustard

¼ tsp. Poppy seeds.

Blend in blender.

While blending, add cold water if it is too oily, until dressing is frothy.

Easy Oil and Vinegar Dressing

1 cup oil, (can substitute Rejuvelac for part)

½ cup apple cider vinegar

¼ cup Nama Shoyu

A 6-second squirt of ketchup

A 2-second squirt of mustard

Shake 30x. Stores in fridge indefinitely.

Creamy French Sprouted Dressing

In blender add:

1 cup of cold pressed oil

½ cup of apple cider vinegar

¼ cup of Kikkoman Soy Sauce or Nama Shoyu (raw soy sauce)

A 6-second squirt of ketchup

A 2-second squirt of mustard

2 Tbsp. raw honey

3 stalks celery

½ red Pepper

¼ small onion

1 sprig Rosemary (optional)

1 clove fresh garlic

1-2 cups red lentil sprouts

Juice of 1 lemon

Blend until smooth. Keeps in the fridge for about a week.

Easy Seed Cheese Dressing

In a small bowl mix:

3 Tbsp. seed cheese

Add "Easy Oil and Vinegar Dressing" until desired consistency

Note: this dressing doesn't keep well because of the living seed cheese.

Mix up one serving at a time.

Serve immediately on your salad.

Mexican Vinaigrette

1 cup olive oil

½ cup fresh lemon juice

½ cup apple cider vinegar

1" ginger, pressed

4 cloves minced garlic

3 Tbsp. Nama Shoyu, or Kikkoman Soy sauce

1 sprig chopped fresh basil

1 sprig chopped fresh cilantro

½ tsp. oregano

¼ red pepper, chopped

½ tsp. cumin

½ raw jalapeno, minced (optional)

Shake and serve. You can blend this too.

Toss for the Mexi Salad, or use as a general salad dressing.

Keeps in the fridge for about 7-10 days.

Sesame Ginger Dressing

2 Tbsp. cold pressed sesame oil

2 Tbsp. brown rice vinegar

3 Tbsp. Rejuvelac or water

2 Tbsp. Nama Shoyu or Kikkoman

1 clove garlic, pressed

½" fresh ginger, pressed

2 Tbsp. fresh lemon juice

3 Tbsp. finely minced sweet onion

Pinch of "Real Salt" (optional)

Mix with a wire whisk or blend.

Sweet and Sour Dressing

½ cup soaked pitted dates blended with:

2 tsp. brown rice vinegar or apple cider vinegar

4 Tbsp. olive oil

1 Tbsp. expeller pressed sesame oil (optional)

3 tsp. Nama Shoyu or Kikkoman (to taste)

4 tsp. mustard (hot mustard is optional)

2 inches of fresh ginger, pressed

1 Umeboshi plum (optional)

¾ cup fresh orange juice

¼ cup fresh lemon juice

4-6 soaked-pitted dates, pure maple syrup or raw honey (to taste).

Blend well. You can add fresh pineapple juice too.

This is good as a salad dressing too.

Pico de Gallo Salsa for Salad

Dice:

3-4 ripe tomatoes

1 bunch green onions

1 fresh jalapeño (or part of it, seeds are optional!)

1 handful cilantro

1 clove garlic (pressed)

Fresh lime juice

Mix together and serve!

This is a great dressing. It is also great as a salsa for your dehydrated chips, a much healthier choice than eating deep-fried tortilla chips that are really hard on the gall bladder.

Sweet Red Pepper Dressing

In a blender add:

1 cup of soaked sunflower seeds

½ red pepper

¼ small red onion

2 cloves garlic

1-2 tsp. cumin

1 Tbsp. Spike (to taste)

¼ tsp. Mexican seasoning

"Real Salt" and pepper (to taste)

Blend well. Lasts 2-3 days.

Sunflower Curry Dressing

¾ cups of soaked sunflower seeds

1 cup of carrot juice

1-3 tsp. curry powder

Dash of Spike

Blend. Use Rejuvelac for desired consistency, more sunflower seeds for thicker dressing.

Mock Thousand Island Dressing (this is not a raw dressing)

½ cup Veganaise (fridge section of the health food store)

1/3 cup ketchup of your choice (to taste)

¼ cup sweet pickle relish

½ tsp. Bubbies fresh horseradish (optional) fridge section of the health food store

Mix together. Use as a salad dressing or:

Use for raw veggies as a dip for steamed veggies

Great for a sauce for burgers

Use as a dip for the raw crackers

Note: This dressing is a transitional food, not a raw food. As you are getting used to the tastes and textures of raw greens and sprouts, you may find this a great help.

Marinated Salads

     A delicious way to enhance any meal is with a marinated salad. The flavors blend so nicely, and marinated salads are especially delicious and healthy when they are served on top of a bed of finely chopped greens. Let them marinate in the fridge for at least an hour before serving. Note: Because of the nature of raw foods and sprouts, salads made with vinegar will only keep for about 24-48 hours before the vinegar begins to break it down.

Sprouted Wheat Berry Tabbouleh
    3 cups sprouted wheat berries
    2 medium tomatoes, chopped
    1 large cucumber, chopped
    5 green onions, thinly sliced
    1 red pepper, thinly sliced
    ½ up fresh parsley, minced
    2 Tbsp. fresh mint, minced
    Mix together with:
    2 Tbsp. olive oil
    3 Tbsp. lemon juice
    ½" pressed fresh ginger

1 clove garlic, pressed

¼ tsp. "Real Salt"

¼ tsp. Spike or onion powder

Chill for 1 hour

Approx: 200 calories, 8 gm protein

Winter Sprout Salad

½ cup each:

>   Garbanzo bean sprouts
>
>   Green lentil sprouts
>
>   Whole green pea sprouts
>
>   Mung bean sprouts
>
>   Sunflower, pea or buckwheat greens, chopped

Coarsely *mince*:

>   ½ small red onion
>
>   1 red pepper
>
>   1 yellow pepper
>
>   ½ large jicama
>
>   1 small yam

Dressing:

>   ¾ cup cold-pressed oil
>
>   ½ cup sweetener (honey, maple syrup, etc.)
>
>   ¾ cup raw apple cider vinegar
>
>   1 clove garlic, minced
>
>   1/8 tsp. cumin
>
>   "Real Salt" and pepper (to taste)

Mix together and pour over salad.

Avocado Recipes

Using avocados as dips or as dressings can cut down on your consumption of oil. Even when you are losing weight, you can still enjoy an avocado every few days, either in a salad or as a dressing.

Choose avocados that are hard to the touch and set them on your counter for a few days. Use them for salads or sandwiches or just plain. You may like them firm or soft to the touch; this is a personal preference. However, if the avocados are very soft, they are at the best stage for blending them in dressings and dips.

Using a sharp knife cut the avocado in half lengthwise beginning at the stem. Take the avocado in both hands and twist along the cut. The avocado will break in half with the pit on one side. Pry out the pit by carefully placing the sharp point of the knife under the pit next to the flesh and flick it out of the cradle. Note: If you are making guacamole, save the pit. Once you place the pit back in the middle of the dip, the avocado thinks that it is still intact and will not brown while you are waiting to eat it!

After you remove the pit, carefully cut diagonal slices, but don't break the tough shell. Then, using a large spoon, scoop out the flesh and fan out the slices on top of your salad. Or you can place the slices on bread or crackers and make an avocado sandwich.

If you are making a dressing or guacamole and don't have a blender, you can use a fork or potato masher to achieve the desired consistency; then you can add other ingredients and whip them together. Avocados are a versatile food and sometimes an acquired taste. Take avocados, when they are still hard, in your backpack or cooler. You want to choose them at a stage that they will ripen in a day or two. You will enjoy the energy that comes from the avocado if you are hiking or playing hard in the wilderness.

Guacamole (great as a Salad Dressing too!)
    4-5 avocados, smashed
    Juice of 1 lime or lemon (to taste)
    ¼ red onion, minced
    1 clove garlic, minced
    Spike or "Real Salt" and pepper (to taste)
Variation: Can be made in a blender adding tomatoes or salsa.

Avocado Dill Sauce or Dressing
    2 avocados
    ½ small cucumber
    1 clove garlic
    4 tomatillos
    ½ tsp. dill seed
    Spike to taste
Blend, using Rejuvelac until desired consistency.

Rejuvelac-Avocado-Dill Dressing
Blend:
    3 avocados

¼ small onion

2-3 cloves fresh garlic

2 tomatillos (optional)

¼ cucumber (optional)

Juice of 1 lime or lemon

½ tsp. dill seed

Add Rejuvelac to desired consistency.

Blend until smooth.

Incredible Avocado Sprout Sandwich

(a transition recipe)

Sprouted Wheat Yeast Bread:

> Spread with Veganaise, stone ground mustard, and
> horseradish (optional)

Layer:

> Avocado, fresh tomato, peppers, sliced zucchini and
> crookneck, grated carrot, sliced red onion, lentil
> sprouts, alfalfa, fenugreek, or any sprouts
>
> Chopped sunflower greens, a lettuce leaf and a slice
> of your favorite pickle

Sprinkle with Spike

Cover with Lemon Tahini dressing and Oil and Vinegar

French Dressing (optional)

Spread Mock Thousand Island Dressing on one side of
the bread (optional)

Take a big bite and eat it over a plate, or

Enjoy open faced and eat it with a fork!

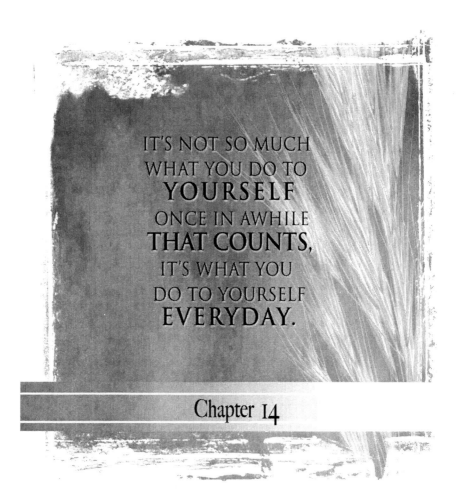

IT'S NOT SO MUCH
WHAT YOU DO TO
YOURSELF
ONCE IN AWHILE
THAT COUNTS,
IT'S WHAT YOU
DO TO YOURSELF
EVERYDAY.

Chapter 14

Make it Happen! Integrating Personal Food Production Daily

When it comes to permanent health, energy or weight management, your daily habits can either make or break you. Forming a new habit takes practice and time, and not deciding to form a habit embraces any excuse. There are myriad justifications to not take care of your body now.

> "I'm too busy. I don't have the money. This takes too much time. I need simplicity in my life. Next month will be a better time to start. I don't really need this right now; I feel well enough."

The list goes on. But procrastination catches up to everyone. As soon as you get that diagnosis that you always feared, as soon as that event comes that you always knew would happen, as soon as things get beyond your control, *then* you are forced to change your course *fast*. But changing course at a critical time can add stress to your already-stressed life. The essential elements of patience and consistency are much more difficult to achieve when life has thrown you a major curve. It is much easier to make the change today when you have the luxury of time. Now is the season to focus on "choice" rather than "fear." Now is the season to have fun with healthy foods and experience the results.

You will discover, as have many others, that adding just a few of these healthy foods to your daily diet can create peace of mind, steady energy, and a wonderful feeling of well being throughout your body. "It makes my cells feel so good!" "I feel as though life is coming at me more slowly, so I can handle it."

Possibly the very thing that you don't think that you have time for is the very thing that will make you *feel* that you have more time. Anything you can do to inspire you to take a look at your own life and engage in your own health and improve the heath of your family is worth the price. Here are some helpful ideas:

Plan ahead. Make a weekly menu every Saturday, Sunday or your day off. Think of your schedule for the coming week and realistically plan *now* how to get you through *then*. If you schedule in this way you will not only find that you have more time, with less moments of desperate feelings of starvation but you will save money by preparing healthy foods ahead of time. You can use the money that you save to purchase other things that might *improve* your long-term health.

Ask yourself this question: "If I stopped buying soda pop, candy, fruit snacks, crackers, frozen quick foods, meat, dairy, or going to the burger joint for lunch everyday and eating out all the time, could I could save money for healthier foods and treatments that would improve my health?"

You may find that as you just "do it" and be willing to learn *as* you are transitioning, the weight will come off, your energy level will gradually rise, the clarity of thought will magically appear, and your health will improve. You never may feel "ready" to start living a healthy lifestyle with commitment. So just start! If you fall off the wagon, just get back on and start again...and again and again. Eventually you will develop the habit of personal lifestyle management. Eating healthy foods will become a happy experience. You may discover that your *life* and your *house* start to become *uncluttered*; you might even want to pursue a new career; you might discover that your attitude about life is more positive, and life's meanings more deep. You might want to start really *living!*

Shop only once a week. Use what food you have in the house and learn to become creative with healthy substitutions. Become a *food mixer*—mix flavors and create your own taste sensations! When you shop, gather! Buy extra seeds, nuts and grains and oils that you are using everyday in your sprouting and gardening.

Sprouting is easy, once you work your own kinks out. Work through the learning curve...*before* a life crisis hits! Get the right equipment, and move things around in your kitchen to give your healthy lifestyle priority. The easier the access to the equipment, the easier the food will be to make. Here are a few ideas and items to accumulate:

• Make sure you have glass quart jars for soaking nuts, seeds, and grains. Typically, you will pour off and store fresh Rejuvelac in glass quart jars in the fridge.

- Buy one or two gallon glass jars for Rejuvelac soaking.
- Purchase a large bowl or pitcher with a pour spout to pour off the finished Rejuvelac.
- Accumulate large rubber bands and twist ties.
- Buy packages of cheesecloth.
- Buy two sprouting trays with lids and dividers. You can always accumulate more, at a later time, as your variety of sprouts expands.
- Purchase a high-speed blender or a *Vita Mix*-type blender to withstand the pressure of the thick fibers and the bulk of raw foods, *and* to create creamy and fluffy textures.
- Purchase an electric or hand-operated grater/slicer. Some delicate veggies and fruit must be grated or sliced by hand. Include a good vegetable peeler.
- Purchase a good set of knives: a wedge knife for chopping, a large serrated blade for watermelon and for large bunches of salad, a paring knife, and a strong cleaver to open baby coconuts. Get a few big chopping blocks.
- Purchase a *Champion Juicer*-type of food processor that can not only juice but also can homogenize or make dough of sprouted and raw foods. Great for pâtés and manna breads.
- Purchase a wheatgrass juicer, either manual or electric. Wheatgrass juice is too fibrous for a normal spin juicer, which doesn't "press" the juice.

- Purchase a food dehydrator, which has a thermostat that can be regulated at 105° F, and has enough solid and mesh dividers for each shelf. If you can, purchase extra shelves so you can dehydrate more for storage.
- Save up and purchase a steam-distilled water purifier to use on a day-to-day basis, or in times of water shortage.
- Purchase some large bowls, a large colander for draining, spoons, airtight storage containers, airtight storage bags, larger storage containers for extra stored nuts, seeds and grains. For easier cleanup, purchase a bottle brush and a thin brush with a handle.
- Be sure to make some cabinet space in your kitchen to store additional dried seeds for everyday use. Also purchase large storage containers for more seeds, nuts and grains that you should store in a dry place, such as in the basement or garage.
- Create a *little* time each day to soak, prepare, and store these healthy foods.

Commitment. Busy days mean you have to be committed and use some ingenuity to dedicate the time to follow this program.

Sprouting:

Soak the seeds at night before going to bed.

First thing in the morning pour the seeds off into the trays, rinse them, let them drain, and allow them sit all day. This should take only 1-2 minutes.

When you come home from work in the evening, rinse and drain the sprouts again, and snack on some. Eat them when the taste is still sweet. Use them in your salads, dressings, sandwiches, or just plain. If they need more time to grow, just keep watering them morning and evening until they are ready.

If you have leftovers, put them in airtight storage bags for about 3-4 days. After that, throw them in some cracker batter in your dehydrator overnight. Have fun!

Crackers:

Crackers are fast and easy, great for on the run. It only takes a few minutes to throw leftover raw foods, wheat or sprouts in the blender with some Rejuvelac, water, or even fresh juices, to create a great taste. Spread the batter on a solid dehydrator sheet then stack it in the dehydrator, and turn it on. That's it! In about 24-36 hours you will have crackers that you can store in airtight bags with a paper towel in the bag. You can eat them at any time!

If you want thicker crackers, pour the batter thicker on the trays, and then dehydrate. After about six hours, turn the sheet over and bend it backwards slightly to

release the cracker. Let the cracker continue to dehydrate for another 12-24 hours so it will be especially
crisp.

Manna breads and cookies:

Make these on a slower day. When you have gath-
ered all the ingredients, start by running the sprouts and
vegetables through the Champion Juicer to make the
dough. Cleanup the juicer immediately before everything gets hard.

Mix all ingredients together and season to taste.

Form into patties or, for cookies, spoon onto mesh
sheets and place them in the dehydrator for about four
hours. Flip over the entire mesh sheet and dehydrate on
the other side for another four hours, or until they are
crisp on the outside and softer on the inside. Use these
softer ones during the upcoming week; store them in
airtight bags in the fridge.

If, after a week, you have leftovers in the fridge, put
them back in the dehydrator until all of the moisture is
gone. Store these like crackers to use for camping, hiking, to grab on the go, or to add to your salad.

Rejuvelac:

Rejuvelac is on a "three-day repeat" cycle. Once the
wheat is ready, the process takes only two minutes.

Just blend two cups of the sprouted wheat with
water for ten seconds then pour it into the gallon glass

jar. Fill the jar with water; cover with cheesecloth and bind with a rubber band, and let it sit on the counter for 6-24 hours or until it starts to smell like unsweetened lemonade.

Holding on to the rubber band, pour the contents through the cheesecloth into a large bowl that has a pour spout. Pour the contents in the bowl into three glass quart jars. Start drinking one of those jars that day, and store the other two jars in the fridge for tomorrow. Drink a quart of the Rejuvelac everyday.

As soon as you pour off the three quarts, soak another two cups of wheat in another glass quart jar to start the next batch of sprouts. You will be ready to make more Rejuvelac in about two days. (If you are making seed cheese you will need about ½ quart of Rejuvelac.)

Seed Cheese:

Seed cheese takes very little time to prepare once you get the hang of it.

After the seeds have soaked overnight, drain the water from the jar and pour into a blender. Add enough Rejuvelac to make a thick paste. Blend it until it becomes smooth (takes about two minutes).

Pour it into a bowl that is lined with three layers of cheesecloth then pull the four corners of the cloth together. Twist it, and bind with a large rubber band.

Using the rubber band, twist the bag around the water faucet so the seed bag can drain over the sink for 6-8 hours while you sleep or while you are at work.

Move the bag to the fridge. Hang the bag from one of the refrigerator shelves; secure it with something like a heavy bottle to keep it from falling. In about six hours you have cheese!

Take the cheese out of the cheesecloth, and place it in an airtight storage container in the fridge for about 7-10 days. Use three tablespoons everyday in your dressings or recipes.

Start another batch, perhaps every other time you make Rejuvelac.

Gather equipment that doesn't require electricity. Be prepared for an emergency.

Suribachi and pestle. A suribachi is a serrated bowl in which you can grind foods with a pestle. These are usually found in Japanese food stores. They are used to make Gomasio. They can be used to grind sprouts into dough, or to grind sprouted wheat a little so it can soak in a gallon glass jar to make the Rejuvelac.

Hanging, tiered solar dehydrator. This can be used in hot weather, in a furnace room or by a wood stove to dehydrate on the solid or mesh sheets. This process takes a little more time, so watch for fermentation.

When you pour the batters and make the patties, think *much thinner.*

Hand-crank wheatgrass juicer. You will use this tool to make wheatgrass juice. It is also good for giving soft berries and vegetables a "homogenized," dough-like texture.

Hand-crank meat grinder. You will use this tool to make dough from sprouted grains, seeds and nuts, if you have no electricity.

Use your creativity and be committed. You'll be surprised at how much you can do with or without electricity and with or without all of the "right" equipment. When you are committed to permanent optimal health, you will have options open up to you to support you in your committed choice. Remember that maintaining and sustaining good health is a most valuable achievement—the foundation to enjoying and accomplishing other life pursuits.

Your adventure has just begun!
May your journey be meaningful!